T0070324

ACCESS
TO
KINGDOM
ANOINTING

GRACE NKANGA

authorHOUSE®

AuthorHouse™
1663 Liberty Drive
Bloomington, IN 47403
www.authorhouse.com
Phone: 1 (800) 839-8640

© 2017 Grace Nkanga. All rights reserved.

No part of this book may be reproduced, stored in a retrieval system, or
transmitted by any means without the written permission of the author.

Published by AuthorHouse 02/18/2017

ISBN: 978-1-5246-6962-1 (sc)
ISBN: 978-1-5246-6961-4 (e)

Library of Congress Control Number: 2017901399

Print information available on the last page.

Any people depicted in stock imagery provided by Thinkstock are models,
and such images are being used for illustrative purposes only.
Certain stock imagery © Thinkstock.

This book is printed on acid-free paper.

Because of the dynamic nature of the Internet, any web addresses or links contained in
this book may have changed since publication and may no longer be valid. The views
expressed in this work are solely those of the author and do not necessarily reflect the
views of the publisher, and the publisher hereby disclaims any responsibility for them.

*Scripture quotations marked KJV are from the Holy Bible, King James Version
(Authorized Version). First published in 1611. Quoted from the KJV Classic
Reference Bible, Copyright © 1983 by The Zondervan Corporation.

*The Living Bible copyright © 1971 by Tyndale House Foundation. Used
by permission of Tyndale House Publishers Inc., Carol Stream, Illinois
60188. All rights reserved. The Living Bible, TLB, and the The Living
Bible logo are registered trademarks of Tyndale House Publishers.

FOREWORD

Hashem has a plan for mankind to return to Him completely before the closure of His plan in the earth. Hashem is faithful and would not judge the world that has not had the opportunity of knowing His glory. Therefore, He said the knowledge of the glory of the LORD must fill the earth as the water covers the sea. Hashem gave me a mandate to redirect His people back to bible basics, because the deceiver has perverted the word and drawn the people out of the Hashem's Kingdom. Especially the disobedience against His command to Honor the seventh day of the week as Hashem's rest. We have left the seventh day and we have been worshiping Hashem on the first day of the week according to human doctrine.

Hashem's mandate to me is first of all to show the image of His Kingdom, so that when we compare with what we are right now, we will be provoked to return to his pattern. As it is written "Show the house to the house that whosoever sees it may run". He has not given me this mandate because I am perfect as at now, rather, as He reveals His word to me daily I am being renewed in my Spirit Man.

I have experienced much opposition in my work with the Lord and am ready to take up any challenge with, the LORD on my side. He called me a "Repairer of the Breach" like Jeremiah and Ezekiel. By His special grace, I was ordained a "Proof Producing Minister" under the Ministry of Dr. Morris Cerullo World Evangelism Ministry. I am also a graduate of the Ohio Christian University with BA in Pastoral Leadership and Ministry. Am a wife and mother of four with six grand-children as at now. Hashem is not a respecter of persons neither does age make a difference. Therefore, I am humbled that Hashem has chosen me to be a Kingdom Global Missionary for Him to hear the word by revelation and his Rhema at His mouth and spread it into the ears of his universal church till they are pricked in the heart and return to Him.

Hashem established me and my prayer partners in Yahweh Global Prophetic Open Heaven Ministries, and joint partners with Yashuah on the right hand of Hashem to bring correction to His church and those who will hearken will be marked as the bride that will rule and reign with Him on His return.

Rev. Grace A. Nkanga (BA)

AWARD: 2015 Global Impact Award

DEDICATION

This book is written in honour of Yahweh, our Father in heaven, maker of heaven and earth. The full breasted one who loves his creation so much that he gave his only begotten son Yashuah Ha Mashiah to redeem us and not only save us but ensure that we enter into His Kingdom where he prepared mansions for us. We will address our Heavenly Father and Jesus Christ in Hebrew language which are Yahweh (YHVH) and Yashuah Ha Mashiah. Written by inspiration of the Holy Spirit and penned by Rev. Grace Nkanga.

I give glory to My Father in Heaven, my Lord Yeshuah Hamashiah the Head of my life and to the Holy Spirit my paraclete who has found it fit to put me in the ministry and to communicate his desire for today's practical Christian walk so that his will should be done on earth as it is in heaven.

Yahweh does not want us to be stuck in the earthly kingdom of Satan after being saved, rather He desires us to be transformed by the renewing of our mind as Yeshuah Hamashiah has taught us by his personal example here in the earth for three and half years.

Now let us learn His pattern, emulate Him and finish the work so that we can enter the mansion prepared for us in His kingdom. He commands us to occupy till He comes.

I also give glory to Yahweh for my daughter Dr. Blessing Akpofure who God used to prophesy to me about amending my priorities in 2003 to put God first in everything in my life. Before then I really believed that I had God first but after that prophesy, I sat back and considered my ways, and I discovered that other things were occupying my heart more than God did. I heeded that word of counsel from the Lord and set my priorities in divine order and today God is pleased to use me because I can now hear and obey him.

I also give glory to God for all my children Dr. Blessing O. Akpofure, (MD) USA, Blossom O. Nkanga (BSc, MBA-MIS) USA, Oton O. Nkanga, Exxon Mobil, Nigeria, Pearl O. Okon BA Banking and Finance Nigeria. They are all born again and walking with the Lord so I had no problem concentrating upon God's calling. With their co-operation I am able to achieve God's full purpose for my life.

I give glory to Yahweh for divinely connecting me with Wayne Persia, my Course Administrator and

Counselor at the Ohio Christian UniversIty in 2011 who willingly proof read this book for me.

I give glory to Yahweh, Yeshua and to the Ruach Ha Khodesh for a timely divine connection with a great Woman of God, Apostle Londen Winters who proof read the final manuscript of this book. I pray God's blessing upon all for their contribution.

God put's someone in our life at a time for a purpose. God brought me into the sphere of Dr. Morris Cerrulo and through his training, authenticated and ordained my ordination of Yahweh. Dr. Morris Cerrulo, ordained me a proof producing minister to show Yahweh's love and deliverance for his people.

I give honour and glory to Yahweh for my Pastor and mentor, Dr. Michelle Corral of Breath of the Spirit Ministry through whose glorious anointing the stronghold that militated against my writing was broken, and now, this book is coming into manifestation. This is a very important part of my destiny, because the LORD had put writing in my heart and I had written many books in the past that were destroyed altogether in the mainstream, including manuscript and I could not put them back together. Some of those books were titled "The blessing of Obedience" and "How to Maintain your deliverance". I pray that the Holy Spirit will bring back the word of those books to my spirit again, because they form a very crucial part of the believer's Christian walk on earth. This particular book "Access into the Kingdom Anointing" also suffered the same hindrance but thank Yahweh for technology and the bondage breaking prayers over my writings. It is finally being published.

ABOUT THE AUTHOR

The LORD Hashem is the Author of this book Access to the Kingdom Anointing. It is at his command that the under-author through His inspiration that she has written this book. The under-author is also the under-CEO of the Yahweh Global Prophetic Open Heaven Ministries founded and inspired by the Holy Spirit. The YGPOHM is Yahweh's personal prophetic Intercessory group who stand to minister as He directs by the Holy Spirit. It was at one of these meetings that the LORD commanded that what He has been teaching the group should be documented for his global Kingdom Citizens to learn from and prepare themselves for the Kingdom work.

The under- Author of the book Access to the Kingdom Anointing is an anointed servant of Hashem with a teaching calling. She is a missionary and has traveled to the Philippines Liberia, Ghana and many countries in Africa. She is a Holy Ghost Student and an astute disciple of Yashuah Hamashiah who taught his disciples to walk as He walked. Yashuah said, "My Father works hitherto and I work" (John 5:17). The LORD Yahweh mandated the author to write this book to draw his creation back to Him. He inspired her to write as the Holy Spirit directs in order to show the way to his people and Yashuah will bring the people unto the Father as they diligently follow His direction. The book "Access to the Kingdom Anointing" is not only an inspirational book which if read under inspiration of the Holy Spirit will provoke a change in the lives of the reader, but it is also written in a way that it can be used in schools as a Text book in Ministry courses. The author acknowledges that without the anointing, the Church cannot make an impact upon the people as Yashuah and the Apostles demonstrated. Therefore the book states clearly the importance for all who aspire towards the Kingdom of Hashem to pay the price like our patriarchs did so that the Heavenly Father will be glorified.

The Executive Author Hashem planned that the words of this book should jolt the church out of complacency and pursue Holiness and Righteousness, without which no man can see Hashem.

AWARDS

In recognition of her work towards global sanctification and impacting the nations for the Kingdom of Hashem as well as provoking a peaceable life for the people before the return of Yashuah, the author was given an award at the 21 Annual Recognitions by the Economic Recovery Institute organized by the Association of Women For African Development based in Chicago, on December 29, 2015.

The Ohio Christian University conferred upon the under Author a Barchelor of Arts degree (cum laude) with speciality in Pastoral Leadership in Ministry. She is also presently pursuing her Masters in Professional Counselling at Liberty University.

PREFACE

This book is designed for use in Christian Colleges and Christian Institutions. For Heavenly Kingdom-minded Christians whose goal is to be Christ-like minded and be adorned for Yashuah our bridegroom.

For all who will walk in Divine Kingdom Authority which Yahweh had predetermined for those that will love eternally and unconditionally.

I wrote this book under inspiration of the Holy Spirit. That being the case, I strongly advise that it should be studied under the inspiration of the Holy Spirit in order to get the best out of it. Our goal is not to give you information or knowledge but to provoke a spiritual transformation of your walk and work in the planet earth while you enjoy the privilege of heavenly Kingdom here in planet earth before transiting to your heavenly home which Yashuah has prepared for you in His Father's house of our Father and our God.

NB. All Scripture quotations are from King James Version and the Living Bible version

THE TABERNACLE OF GOD

The Tabernacle is made of Shittim Wood and overlayed with gold and contains the Golden Ark in which the Ark of Testimony and the rod of Aaron that budded was placed. (Exo. 25:9 – 22). The Mercy Seat of Gold with two Cherubims sitting on the Ark of Testimony and the glory of the LORD appears between when the LORD meets with us.

> "Behold the Tabernacle of God is with men and He will dwell with them, and they shall be his people and God himself shall be with them and be their God". "Know ye not that ye are the temple of God." We are the dwelling place of God and our temples must be holy, righteous and sanctified unto the LORD for the Godhead (Father Son and Holy Ghost to dwell in according to John 14:20 – 23 and Revelation 21:3. That is the reason Yashuah Hamashiah said the Kingdom of God is within us. (Mark 14: 58, 1 Corinthians 3:16.)

Every aspect of the magnificent edifice of the Tabernacle is relevant to our spiritual status in God and in his Kingdom. The symbol of the Tabernacle is expected to be reproduced in the life of every believer according to the pattern set down by Hashem to Moses. Yeshua Hamashiah has produced and demonstrated the characteristic thereof. It is a mystery that shall be revealed to every seeking heart as they read this book and others that will follow. Details and relevance of the Tabernacle to our lives will be written in our new book by God's special grace.

God bless you as you study this book and take heed to its contents in Yashuah Hamashiah's matchless name. Amen.

CONTENTS

I adjure all who read this book to use it as a study book. This is actually a course of teaching on the whole power behind our success into the Kingdom of Yahweh and how to walk in it here on earth.

CHAPTER 1

Understanding the KINGDOM and the Anointing

And the seventh angel sounded; and there were great voices in heaven, saying, "The kingdoms of this world are become **the kingdoms** of our Lord, and of his Christ; and he shall reign forever and ever" (Rev. 11:15)

"For in him dwelleth all the fullness of the Godhead bodily". And ye are complete in him, which is the head of all principality and power" (Col 2:9, 10). This scripture makes is clear that all the attributes of Yashuah Hamashiah is complete in us. Therefore in reality, we should be operating in all the anointing that is in Yashuah Hamashiah. But we know the price that He paid for it, we must also pay the price by dying to our flesh, allowing the Holy Spirit to flow in and through us. Yashuah said, "Flesh and blood cannot inherit the Kingdom of Yahweh neither corruption inherit incorruption." (1 Cor. 15:50) The scripture has declared it, but it is not sufficient for us to believe it, claim it, receive it and walk in it. In order to walk in it, we must follow the pattern set out for us by our Master Yashuah Hamashiah. That is why He said we must deny ourselves, take up our cross and follow him. (Matt. 16:24)

The kingdom is the estate of kings where all the kings dwell. In this case we are talking about the Kingdom of Yahweh and of His Christ (Rev. 12:10). It is written, "the Kingdom of heaven is at hand" because we as kings and priests who have chosen to sanctify ourselves shall have the privilege of being the dwelling place of the Godhead. We are the hands, legs, eyes, ears and mind of the Godhead here on earth. We are the vessels that will bring the will of God and his kingdom to reign here in the earth as it is in heaven. (Matt. 6:9,10) We are being equipped with knowledge through the revelation in the bible and spiritually explanation in this book. Many believers still do not understand that the book of revelation is all about the prophecy of Yeshuah's reign on earth with his bride. The revelations are all about the end-time and the disaster which is to come upon all who do not submit themselves to Yeshuah's adornment. All believers are expected to walk in the spirit as it is written in Rom. 8:1a, believers who are walking in the flesh and carnality are under condemnation. Therefore, believers are warned to put on the mind of Yashuah and buy of Him gold tried in fire to prove themselves ready as the five wise virgins. The five foolish virgins are likened to those believers who are walking in the flesh. Yashuah will tell them in the end, "Verily I say unto you, I knew you not". (Matt.25:12) Therefore, we must take heed to the prophecies of the bible and go back to the root of the bible.

The bride of Yashuah is to drive away the prince of this world from their lives in order to get rid of the Satan and his cohorts from this world. "And the seventy returned again unto him saying, Lord even the devils are subject unto us through thy name. And He said unto them, "I beheld Satan as lightning fall from heaven. Behold, I give unto you power to thread upon serpents and scorpions if you drink any poisonous thing, it shall not hurt you." (Lk. 10: 17 − 19) We must be made compatible with Yeshuah Hamashiah for his mighty light and power to shine and drive out the adversary out of our lives and out of the world. Besides having the power of attorney through His name, compatibility to His nature will enhance the supernatural in our lives and ministry. We cannot harbor the things of the devil and expect that the devil will be afraid of us and obey our command. Therefore, we must prune out every resemblance of the characteristics of the devil out of our lives so that Yeshuah will have the pre-eminence over our lives, and we will fulfill the mandate of Yashuah in our lives and ministry. Yeshuah said that in that day, we will know that He is in the Father Yahweh and Yahweh is in him and we shall be in Him and He in us, then if we love Him and keep his commandment, we shall be loved of His Father and He will manifest Himself to us. (John 14:20, 21). As we love and obey Yashuah's commandment, we make our temples compatible for the Godhead to dwell in and operate through. Yeshuah Hamashiah has given us the power of attorney to function in LK. 10:19, yet we are unable to fully operate with that power because we still have some of the Satan's attribute in our lives. Remember that Yashuah Hamashiah told the disciples and us that the Prince of the World comes and he shall find nothing in Him. (John 14:20) In this book we will show us those things in our lives that challenge our power of attorney, the adversary who is resisting us is not operating from outside of us, he operates through our mind, will, emotion and desire in the same way that the Godhead operates through believers who are in tune with Him in the Spirit; "For God is Spirit and they that worship him must worship him in Spirit and in Truth". (John 4:23). Amen. This means walking in the Spirit so that we can make connection with Yahweh. In effect, walking in the Spirit will cause us not to walk in our carnality because carnality is enmity against Yahweh and we cannot do godly things. The ministry of Yashuah Hamashiah is messianic by nature to save the soul of man which is our mind, will, emotion and desire; so two kingdoms are fighting over your soul. Christ came to save man's soul but the devil is fighting to destroy man's soul. This is the crux of man's life and we have a choice to choose life with Christ or death with the devil. It is not enough to confess Christ for salvation, and continue with the devil attributes in our lives, we must come to the point of being fully sanctified unto Christ then the ministry will be manifested in our lives because that will lead us into the Kingdom of Heaven where we were meant to be. Yashuah's real purpose is to make us a proof of his ministry as we aspire tenaciously to become the king/priest which he has declared unto us. Our seats are empty in the Kingdom, when we overcome the devil's hold in our lives, we will fill those seats in the Kingdom of Yahweh. As long as the devil has a hold upon our soul (Mind, will, emotion, and desire), the devil still has us bound to the kingdom of the world and the Kingdom of Yahweh is not within our reach.

The Anointing:

Yashuah Hamashiah is the perfecter of all things so with the Power of Attorney, He left with us also an anointing for us to function with in John 17:22, He left us the glory which our Father Abba Yahweh gave him. He left the glory with us to function in his stead and He said, "Occupy till I come". (Luke 19:13b) Kings and Priests cannot function without anointing, therefore He commanded us to wait for the promise (power of the Holy Spirit and the anointing) in Acts. 1:8, to empower us to witness of him and the power and Spirit came down upon us in Acts. 2:1 − 4; the Spirit is the anointing. We will speak more elaborately on this in later chapters.

Now that you understand what the Kingdom of God is and what the anointing is, you ought to be determined within your heart to choose the Kingdom of Yahweh and not the church realm. Believers in the church have encompassed the religious house long enough (Deut. 2:3,4). Let us take steps to walk in the mind of Yashuah Hamashiah so that we can gain the Kingdom. Yashuah never worked alone, he worked as He saw His Father work, He spoke as He heard His father speak and this is

5

the pattern that His bride should follow. The only hope to gain access into the Kingdom of Yahweh and His Mashiach is to follow the pattern He has set for us even from the time of Moses represented by Yashuah.

a.   Circumcision of our hearts of flesh:

This circumcision is not a natural circumcision but a spiritual one which Yashuah refers to in John 3: 5 as being baptized in water and the spirit. Yashuah stated very clearly that we can only **see** the kingdom, if we are **baptized in water**. But in verse 5, Yashuah specified, that "Verily, verily, except a man be born of **water and of the spirit**, he cannot **enter** the Kingdom of GOD. In other words, when we are baptized in water, it opens up our hearts to the revelation of Yashuah Hamashiah, and then when we are baptized in the Spirit, then we enter into the realm of the Spirit where the Godhead is and we can relate with the Godhead.

What does it mean to be baptized of the Spirit? This is the circumcision of our hearts, because when the spirit comes upon us, our hearts are transformed from the worldly condition to a divine nature, (Godly nature and likeness of God). It is at this point that the plan and purpose of God to create man in his image AND LIKENESS is being fulfilled. This experience is only an initial deposition of the Spirit of transformation and we are expected to continue to let the Holy Spirit prompt us and direct our paths and lives unto righteousness. Hitherto in Gen. 1:27, God created man in his image while likeness was suspended waiting for man to come to full realization of who we are in God and to willingly surrender ourselves to be changed into His likeness. We do not know what we look like now, but when he doth appear, we shall be like him. "**1Jn 3:2:** Beloved, now are we the sons of God, and it doth not yet appear what we shall be: but we know that, when he shall appear, we shall be like him; for we shall see him as he is. Transformation is not inherited, it is acquired through our willingness to renew our minds by the word of Yahweh according to Rom. 12:1,2. We can achieve the status of transformation only as we allow his word to break and restructure our heart. It is imperative that we be sensitive to the voice and power of the Holy Spirit. We must yield to the Holy Spirit and let him have his way. We are the clay and He is the porter, and as we yield to Him, He causes our hearts to become more supple and pliable for his word to indwell deeply and we shall be rooted and grounded in Christ and put on His mind until our minds are totally renewed to conform with the likeness of Yashuah and think His thoughts and do His will. "And every man that hath this hope in him purifieth himself, even as he is pure". (1Jn. 3:3) That means dying to our flesh so that the word can have access into our heart. When a believer gets to this point, the Christ-like life is birthed and perfection sets in. For, we must be perfect because He is perfect.

b. Purity is one of Yashuah's natural attributes.

We are expected to possess this attribute also. God told Moses, "You must be holy unto me for I the Lord I am Holy" (Lev. 19:2). The domain of God is holy and everyone who desires to enter into his presence must be holy, first judicially then experientially and positionally.

Judicially means that by faith in the shed blood, we have been made pure, and we have received Yashuah as our Lord and Saviour and we get baptized. From the status being born again, we apply the word as soap to wash our hearts like soap, and walk according to the word. We do exactly what the word commands and we follow Christ in the Spirit. Then we start experiencing the effect and power of the word and start experiencing purification in our hearts. Furthermore, at this point we are so caught up with Christ's holiness that we cannot habour any evil in our hearts. There are various measures that we have to observe to experience purification. Obviously, we are being confronted daily by challenging situations, we must rest assured that the Spirit of Christ in us is working on our behalf to overcome them all because Christ Yashuah has already overcome the devil for us and through our experiences and tenacity in faith to the truth, we also overcome our flesh, (mind, emotions, desires and will) which is our soul as we mentioned hitherto. These confrontations are our testing, they will surely, and the way respond or deal with the test will determine our victory or failure. When we overcome with love, mercy and joy in the Lord, we will be immoveable in all ways, we can now say that we are positionally purified, and stand firm before the Lord without compromising with our flesh. One way to constantly check our heart is by the scripture in Php. 4:8 which says, "Finally, brethren, whatsoever things are true, whatsoever things are honest, whatsoever things are just, whatsoever thing are lovely, whatsoever things are of good report; if there be any virtue, and if there be any praise, think on these things." When we constantly check our activities and our lives with this scripture, no evil can lodge in our hearts because it is written, "For from within out of the heart of men proceed evil thoughts, adulteries, fornications, murders, theft, covetousness, wickedness, deceipt lasciviousness, an evil eye, blasphemy, pride, foolishness. All these evil things come from within, and defile the man." Again, it is written, "The heart of man is deceitful above all things, and desperately wicked: who can know it?" (Jer. 17:9) Yahweh formed Adam (man) and kept him in the garden to tend it. Yahweh provided him with a river from Eden which parted into four streams of rivers to water the garden and bring forth fruit for him and commanded him to tend the garden. (Gen. 2:7 − 15). This garden was Yahweh's fellowship place with Adam in the cool of the day. This garden of Eden is a type and shadow of man's heart. Man is to tend and protect his heart from evil defilements, so that only thoughts of Yahweh and good can abide in man's heart. A pure heart in man's temple is Yahweh's dwelling place where the Godhead will come and dwell in the time of the Kingdom of Yahweh coming into the earth. (John

14:20, 21, Col. 3:16, Rev. 21:3). Yahweh is now drawing us unto him to repair the altar which Adam destroyed (our heart), so that He can come into fellowship with us again. So, we see that a pure heart filled with the word (water from his presence) will open an access to the Godhead to not only fellowship with us but abide in and with us. This is a mystery, the Kingdom of Yahweh is with and within us, but there is a price to pay to be able to access His presence, and be one with and in Him.

OBSERVATIONS AND VIEW POINTS

1.1 *Some people find it difficult to understand the Hebrew scripture (Old Testament), so they would rather stick with the New Testament. After the exposition of this first chapter. What is your view?*

1.2 *How does the Hebrew Scripture help you to understand the whole gospel of Yeshuah Hamashiach?*

1.3 *Does it punctuate your need for the anointing more than the New Testament or does it complement it?*

1.4 *Can the anointing be achieved just by claiming the promise? Give supporting scriptures.*

1.5 *What is the pre-requisite for the anointing? Give a supporting scripture.*

1.6 What is the purpose of the anointing on Kings in the Hebrew Testament?

1.7 What does the Kingdom anointing demand of the kingship that Yashuah appointed us into and how does it differ from King David's anointing?

CHAPTER 2

Understanding the Kingdom Anointing?

This is the anointing upon kings. Jesus made us kings and priests unto God and our father. Jesus is the King of kings and Lord of lords. And hast made us to our God kings and priests: and we shall reign on the earth." (Rev 5:10) Yashuah was anointed with the Holy Ghost and with Power from on high to do the work of a King over the kingdoms of kings. David was anointed as a King with a vial of oil. Prophets of old were anointed, Moses was anointed with the anointing of fire by God himself in the burning bush therefore the glory was so heavy on him that the people could not look upon his face and he had to cover his face.

* Yashuah Ha Mashiach our King has made us believers in him kings and priests. We cannot be kings without the anointing or platform, therefore, Yashuah is teaching us to understand who we really are, and is admonishing us to walk in the anointing. No King can function without a portfolio and power. Kings command

power, they do not demand it. They command that power by virtue of the indwelling operational power. This anointing is personal and is acquired as we relate with him and walk by his abiding word and power according to John 15. As kings, we have a kingdom in Yahweh's kingdom extended to the earth. As it were, we have become an antagonist of the Prince of the air who rules over the earth at this present time. Therefore, we must command authority over the activities of the earth which are directed by the Satan in our minds, wills, emotions and desires. These components incidentally are part of our bodies, so primarily, as kings we must command authority over members of our bodies and die to our flesh, then our Spiritual authority becomes effective and the Satan is deprived of his authority over our lives. It is the Kingdom anointing in our lives that expresses Yahweh's power in our lives through our works just like the exceeding great power demonstrated by Yashuah in the letter to the Ephesians.

> "And what is the exceeding greatness of his power to us-ward who believe according to the working of his mighty power" (Eph 1:19)

> "Now unto him that is able to do exceeding abundantly above all that we ask or think, according to the power that worketh in us". (Eph 3:20)

This anointing does not come cheaply, it comes through steadfast prayer and intercessions and a longing and desire for the manifestation there of according to Eph. 1:19 and Eph. 3:20. This exceeding great and mighty power in Yeshuah Hamashiach which he has endowed us with is manifested as we die to our flesh gradually. This power is supposed to work in us as we yield ourselves to him. Yeshuah is able, abundantly able to cause us to walk and work in this power that dwells in Him waiting to be manifested through us. Amen.

a.   Mosaic Priestly/Prophetic Anointing

Moses was anointing directly by Yahweh on Mount Sinai with a peculiar anointing of Fire from El Elohim standing in the LORD's Presence. Moses got a double Anointing as it were from El Elyon and received a Prophetic anointing also. How wonderful it will be to be anointed directly by El Elyon and receive Prophetic anointing and the knowledge of El Elyon's voice personally. This is what we will also achieve, if we accept to experience being in the presence of El Elyon all the time. He is demanding us to come into his presence and have sweet fellowship with Him so He can impart His Glory upon us. Moses's experience is recorded in Exo. 34: 29 – 35; he was transformed by the glory of the presence of El Elyon so that he developed a very meek and quiet Spirit that enabled him to lead a stiff-necked rebellious Isreal.

"And it came to pass when Moses came down from Mount Sinai (with the two tables of testimony in Moses's hand, when he came down from the mount) that Moses knew not that the skin of his face shone, while he talked with him. And when Aaron and all the children of Israel saw Moses, behold, the skin of his face shone, and they were afraid to come nigh him. And Moses called to them; and Aaron and all the rulers of the congregation returned to him; and Moses talked with them. And afterward all the children of Israel came nigh: and he gave them in commandment all that the LORD had spoken with him in Mount Sinai. And till Moses had done speaking with them, he put a veil on his face. But when Moses went in before the LORD to speak with him, he took the veil off, until he came out. And he came out and spoke to the children of Israel *that* which he was commanded. And the children of Israel saw the face of Moses, that the skin of Moses's face shone: and Moses put the veil upon his face again, until he went in to speak with him" (Exo 34:29 -35)

This word is not a myth, it is the word of God and if Moses was faithful in his calling to the house as a servant and Yashuah was faithful as a Son, and they both fulfilled their calling, part of which Joshua walked and fulfilled the actual entering into the promised land, we can and must also fulfill the part of the prophesies that is meant for us to fulfill and there is a price to pay and a pattern that we must follow. We have to walk under the same anointing that Moses and Yashuah walked in, in order to fulfill prophesies. There is a glorious transforming anointing that the world cannot understand which God is releasing in this end time, to equip his body for the Kingdom work. This anointing demands seeing beyond the natural into the supernatural. This Kingdom anointing demands seeing as God sees and walking as God/Yashuah walked in this earth. This is why the word says in Rom. 8:19-22 "They are waiting for us". We must arise and the nations will flow to our arising and shining. Isa. 60: 1 – 4.

We know how Moses achieved this anointing, and how Yashuah achieved this anointing. This anointing will come through walking in willingness, obedience, faith and trust in God and his finished work on the cross. Yashuah said "occupy till I come"; how are we going to occupy? The LORD said "not by power, not by might, but by my Spirit says the Lord." (Zech, 4:6) We must occupy by the Spirit of the Lord. We must die to our flesh and carnality and awake to Elohim's righteousness. The supernatural realm cannot be accessed through our thoughts or observation, it can only be achieved by extraordinary radical faith in Elohim and the finished work of Yashuah on the cross. Above all, we must speak those things that are not as though they are and speak our way into the supernatural.

b. The High Priest Offering Atonement Before the Ark of God's Presence

The duties of a High Priest during the era of Moses included pouring the ashes before Hashem to burn before His presence. These ashes represent the tearful prayers of the Saints. This work has not ceased. The New Testament priest still performs this operation daily in the temple of Elohim. The High Priest pours incense before Elohim and pours the anointing oil for the fire to continue burning in the Holy of Holies. The incense represents the prayers of saints that are continually being presented before Elohim by our High Priest Yeshuah Hamashiach. Though, Yashuah Hamashiach finished this work when He offered his blood at the cross and took it up after resurrection and placed it in the Ark of Testimony for a perpetual token of atonement. (Heb. 7;25-27) He is sitting at the right hand of Our Father eternally making intercession for us as our High Priest in Heaven. We his joint heirs and king priests aught also to join him in the Spirit realm continually interceding for the Church and his universe here in the earth. This is the duty that Yashuah is calling us into. He said we are joint heirs with Him and king priests as He is. Therefore He prayed to the Father that He wishes that we should be with Him where He is that we may behold His glory. (John 17:24) This is the whole duty of His Prophetic

Intercessors, and we in Yahweh Global Prophetic Open Heaven Ministries, are steadfastly continuing in this joint-heirship with the High Priest duty. Unfortunately, the 21st Century Prophets, pray and minister for filthy lucre, and many others do not want to fully obey the LORD to dwell in His presence. This is the whole purpose of the LORD for asking me to write this book in order to draw the prophets and saints of Hashem who are joint-heirs with Yashuah back to faithfulness. Hashem is hungry for our righteousness unto Him. Sometime ago, as we were waiting before the LORD, in prayer, He said, "Faithfulness, Righteousness, and Holiness is all He is asking from us." Our Patriarchs were totally devoted to the duties that Hashem called them into.

OBSERVATIONS AND VIEWPOINTS

2.1   What is the anointing in the New Testament?

2.2   What part does the breath of God play in our lives and in our walk with God?

2.3   What part does the Holy Spirit play in our lives and ministry?

2.4   Unto whom are the gifts of the Spirit given?

2.5   Who can manifest the power of the Holy Spirit?

2.6   How can the church be revived again?

2.7   What is the Mosaic Anointing?

2.8   How can we liken the Mosaic Anointing with the Baptism by fire in *Acts. 2:1?*

2.9   *Are we not expected to be transformed by the Baptism by Fire w?*

2.10 Why was Moses face shining so much that the people of Israel were afraid to look on his face?

2.11 What should we do to be transformed? Give relevant scripture in theHebrew (Old) Testament and New Testament.

2.12 What makes Moses Anointing prophetic? Give scriptures.

CHAPTER 3

Understanding the Diverse Kinds of Anointings and Manifestations?

There are three types of Anointing:

a.   Kingly Anointing (1 Sam. 10:1 and 2 Sam. 2:4,7)

El Elyon anoints certain persons as kings over nations for the purpose of ruling over the nations according to his divine rules, and precepts. He anoints kings to bestow upon them authority to rule in his stead here in the earth. He originally planned to be the only ruling King over his creation and He still is, these kings whom He has anointed to rule on his behalf are only temporal and they take instructions from him. He anointed Saul son of Kish as Captain over Israel and gave him a prophet to guide him through prophetic words directly from El Elyon. The New Testament kings have two anointing, kingly and priestly anointing for Yashuah has made us to be kings and priest unto El Elyon Our Father. (Rev. 1:6)

The Old Testament kings only had a kingly anointing and a prophet of El Elyon assigned to them. The prophet Samuel was King Saul's prophet.

> "Then Samuel took a vial of oil, and poured it upon his head, and kissed him, and said, Is it not because the LORD hath anointed thee to be captain over his inheritance." (1Sa 10:1).

Saul was drunken with power and he mistreated the people of El Elyon and would not wait on Him for instructions nor obey His commandments, so El Elyon removed him and replaced him with a man after his own heart as king over Israel. This is the pattern of the church today and El Elyon is displeased with the church and is now charging us to return to the bible standards and learn His ways. We will learn here in 1 Sam. 16:14, the reason why the church has become such a failure, and seemingly powerless. The reason is that when the glory of El Elyon departs from any local church and Ichabud sets in, automatically, the negative Spirit takes over as we see here in the case of Saul son of Kish. <u>The spirit of El Elyon left him and an evil Spirit came upon him. (1Sa 16:14) "But the Spirit of the LORD departed from Saul, and an evil spirit from the LORD troubled him."</u> Beloved blood purchased people of El Elyon, once we are anointed, we must be careful to walk as David, Moses and Jesus walked so as to walk all the way into the Kingdom of El Elyon and His Christ Yeshuah. If we fall, the devil takes over and everything we do brings evil and death upon those we rule over. The kings and Priests of Yahweh have to realize that they are not anointed for themselves, rather they anointed for the work of the Kingdom and the objects of the Kingdom. Yeshuah said in John 17:19, "And for their sakes I sanctify Myself, that they also may be sanctified by the truth." This is to say that Yashuah walks by the truth as a matter of fact so that we will not find it strange but also walk in the truth to exemplify our Christianity to others who watch us and wish to emulate us as we also emulate Yashuah Hamashiach our Master. Yashuah taught us everything by examples, He never taught what He would not do Himself. King Saul walked totally contrary to the Word and was disobedient even to the voice of El Elyon, therefore He departed from him and gave him an evil Spirit. All believers and Saints of the Most High must imperatively obey His commandments and walk in His ways so we will be able to access the Kingdom and stand before Elohim's presence.

El Elyon sent Samuel the Seer to anoint David, King over Israel because king Saul failed.

> "Then Samuel took the horn of oil, and anointed him in the midst of his brethren: and the Spirit of the LORD came upon David from that day forward. So Samuel rose up, and went to Ramah." (1Sam 16:13)

David suffered very much as a king without a platform or throne after his anointing by Samuel, but his heart was right, he considered Saul was anointed of Yahweh and he would not do any harm to his adversary Saul who pursued after his life to destroy him. This thing pleased El Elyon and He avenged for David by himself. Then He filled the heart of His people (the men of Judah) to anoint David and install him in his throne. Of David purity heart endeared him to El Elyon as well as the people of Judah. We also as kings are expected to please El Elyon in all our ways and thoughts. We must love all people even our adversaries and let El Elyon avenge for us because vengeance belongs to Him. Leaders whose hearts are pure do not need to demand authority, their character just commands favor and authority for them. The people of Judah loved their king David and they fought for him.

"And the men of Judah came, and there they anointed David king over the house of Judah. And they told David, saying, *That* the men of Jabeshgilead *were they* that buried Saul". (2 Sam 2:4) This is a second anointing upon David as King.

David pleased God in all his ways in that he never did anything or took any decision without God's perfect permission. He always sought God's face by the Urim and Thummim for God's perfect will. The Urim and Thummim are lights on the breastplate of the priest for lights and perfection to know God's perfect will in any situation brought before God. The Urim and Thummim is the means of discernment to the Old Testament Priest.

23

The Holy Spirit dwells in the New Testament Priest. Through the gift of the Holy Spirit dwelling in the New Testament Priest, he is able to discern and have prophetic insights and operate spiritual gifts. This is the pattern of kingship that Yahweh desires from his Priests. Yahweh does not want kings and priests that will overthrow Him and take over the rulership over His creation. We can see from David's life that he was a cultural king and so he had to consult with a Priest "Abiathar" in order to know the mind of Yahweh. He did not take laws into his hands and try to occupy the priest's position as king Saul did. A lot of the pastors and priests of Yahweh today are usurping authority over Yashuah Hamashiach by not obeying the Holy Spirit's direction. Yahweh sent the Holy Spirit to empower us to work the priestly work as we listen and hearken to his voice and direction. Even our Master Yashuah does not do anything that He has not heard His Father command. According to John 5:17 "As I see my Father work I work". We must emulate our Master Yashuah in all ways.

    b.   Priestly Anointing (Exo. 29:7 and Melchizedek Anointing. (Acts 10:38)

AARONIC PRIESTHOOD

"Then shalt thou take the anointing oil, and pour it upon his head, and anoint him. And thou shalt bring his sons, and put coats upon them. And thou shalt gird them with girdles, Aaron and his sons, and put the bonnets on them: and the priest's office shall be theirs for a perpetual statute: and thou shalt consecrate Aaron and his sons.

And thou shalt cause a bullock to be brought before the tabernacle of the congregation: and Aaron and his sons shall put their hands upon the head of the bullock. And thou shalt kill the bullock before the LORD, by the door of the tabernacle of the congregation. And thou shalt take of the blood of the bullock, and put it upon the horns of the altar with thy finger, and pour all the blood beside the bottom of the altar." (Exo 29:7 -12)

The Aaronic or Levitical priesthood anointing is very different from the Kingly anointing or the Melchizedek Anointing. Part of the Levitical priestly anointing includes the anointed priest placing their hands on the head of a bullock thereby passing their sins over upon the scapegoat as their sin offering before it is killed and the blood sprinkled upon the horn of the altar for sanctification. The blood is a vital part of the process. It signifies the death of the priest to earthly lusts and cravings, it signifies that the priest is perpetually sold out unto the service of God until death. But this is not a one-time event, yearly this sacrifice has to be observed for a re-consecration. This is the priest's offering by fire. The Levitical Priesthood is not connected with the Holy Spirit at any point, but they just believe by faith unto perfection because it is an oath of service given by Yahweh. Yashuah is The New Testament sin-offering for man and this was fulfilled once and for eternity. Unfortunately, this grace has been misused because even after receiving Yashuah as Saviour, some believers feel they can continue in their old ways of life and persist in careless living. Old Testament Priests honored holiness and righteous towards Yahweh and preached it to kings and families without compromise. Old Testament Priests honoured family worship as Yahweh spoke in Deut. 6:7. Holiness and Righteousness are vital pre-requisites to the New Testament Anointing.

Melchizedek Priesthood Anointing:

> "How, God anointed Jesus of Nazareth with the Holy Ghost and with power: who went about doing good, and healing all that were oppressed of the devil; for God was with him". (Act 10:38)

Yeshuah Hamashiah our High Priest fulfilled the part of the slain bullock as our sin offering at the cross. That part of the shedding of blood was fulfilled on the way to Calvary and the blood was poured out upon the altar at the cross. The real anointing was done at his baptism.

"And Jesus, when he was baptized, went up straightway out of the water: and, lo, the heavens were opened unto him, and he saw the Spirit of God descending like a dove, and lighting upon him:

And lo a voice from heaven, saying, This is my beloved Son, in whom I am well pleased." (Mat 3:16, 17).

After Yeshua was baptized in river Jordan, as he stepped out of the water the Holy Spirit descended upon him and declared, "This is my son in whom I am well pleased". This is the power of Jehovah that made his anointing powerful and different from any other. Paul records it in Acts. 10:38, as the power that moved him to heal the sick raise the dead and do wondrous things everywhere he went. Yashuah told the disciples and us to wait until we receive the promise of God from on high to anoint and equip us for service. (Acts. 1:8). We believers are being anointed and equipped for the service of the Kingdom of El Elyon and his Mashiach as we willingly submit ourselves to undergo the training that Jesus demonstrated for us all the way from ministry to the judgment seat, and condemnation to death by hanging. This is all part of the offering by fire that every believer priest must offer to qualify for the priesthood. Thanks to Yahweh the anointing prepares and enables us to bear through to the end. But there are some of us who have merchandised the anointing, and used it for filthy lucre. This might seem contradictory to the word that says, that Yashuah has made us kings and priests unto Jehovah our Father. We must remember that Yashuah said the prince of the air cometh and hath nothing in him. (John 14:30) This means that there is no attribute of Satan or characteristics of the world in Him at all. He is holy and righteous. Likewise must all believers be in order to have a part in the Kingdom. Also, Yashuah said "Flesh and blood cannot inherit the Kingdom of God".

c.   Anointing for Sanctification (Num.8:1 - 26)

The book of Numbers chapter 8 is devoted to the preparation, consecration and dedication of the Aaronic priesthood. In verses 10 – 12, we see an astonishing thing where the Israelites lay hand on the Levites and the Levites lay their hands on the bullock and the bullock is offered unto God. And Aaron and his sons use the Levites as their offering. The whole issue here is that blood had to be offered for dedication and sanctification for service and only the Levites were qualified to serve God and they had to sanctify themselves with the bullocks while Aaron and his sons passed their sins upon the Levites. All these processes were completed and fulfilled in and by Yashuah Hamashiach for us, so we do not have to go through all that sanctification process anymore, but sanctification is not negated. All that we need to do to be sanctified unto Yahweh for His service, is to fulfill all the processes of being born again and filled with the Holy Spirit. Yeshuah was our lamb of sacrifice, and the Holy

Spirit is our sanctifier for service. There is an anointing that flows from the Holy Spirit to us as we enter into sanctification and dedication.

The anointing of Yahweh is His glory which he puts upon his children who separate themselves from the pollution of the world to serve him in spirit and in truth. When Yahweh puts his anointing upon you (the Saints) the world (darkness) cannot approach unto the anointing because the anointing is light and darkness cannot comprehend it. The anointing destroys yokes of bondages. When the glory that was upon Moses, his own people could not look upon his face because it glowed and they were afraid. (Exo. 34:28 – 30). Joshua was also anointed and the Lord told him saying; "Henceforth there shall no man be able to stand before you" (Josh.1:5b). The anointing of Yahweh separates us unto genuine divine greatness. The anointing is the glory of Yahweh and the glory of Yahweh is his presence. Moses told Yahweh, "Show me your glory (face) and Yahweh responded "you cannot see my face but I will put my hand upon your face and pass by you and you will only see my back". If seeing the back of Yahweh is so glorious that it could slay Moses, how much more powerful would seeing the face of Yahweh be!

Yashuah our Messiah was anointed with the Holy Spirit and with power. Anointing is POWER, because the Holy Spirit is the power of God. Yashuah made us believers, kings and priests unto our God, and "WE

SHALL REIGN ON EARTH". Reigning on earth as kings is the issue of discussion in this book. The whole purpose of Salvation and Redemption work is to take back the dominion that was rightfully ours and the Satan stole it from Adam through deception. Therefore, through the wisdom that Yashuah gives us to walk in the Holy Spirit, we will be able to snatch back our dominion because Satan cannot deceive us any more to play around in the church with our fleshly lust. All fleshly lusts must be crucified so that the Holy Ghost can have his way in us. The flesh is Satan's workshop, so when we crucify it, the Holy Spirit starts operating in and through us to establish Yahweh's plans in the earth. When we crucify our flesh and the Holy Spirit works through us, it will be the Spirit of the Most High working through us and not us, though we are the physical vessels through whom the Godhead is ruling and reigning in this earth.

> "And hast made us unto our God kings and priests: and we shall reign on the earth" (Rev 5:10)

Yeshuah Maschiach is an embodiment of the glory and power of Yahweh, so we who have believed in him and received him as our King and our High Priest have become kings and priests in him. We then have both the kingly and priestly anointing upon us. The BIG BUT is "Reigning on earth".

➢ Have we been made to be kings and priests by the King of kings? YES
➢ Are we actually ruling and reigning now? NO
➢ Are we walking and working as priests according to his teaching? NO
➢ Are we exercising the authority and dominion that is our right with proof? NO

This is the purpose of this book. Please let the content of this book provoke you into practicing what you have been empowered to be through your faith in the risen Lord, our Maschiach. We can only work as He commands when we obey and hearken to his voice. OBEDIENCE IS THE KEY TO OUR MANIFESTATION. Yeshuah obeyed every word of Yahweh and overcame the Satan by the same word. So also, the Saints of Yahweh must be obedient unto the death of our flesh and the resurrection of life in the Holy Spirit. The election of the king priests is through sanctification by the Holy Spirit and the preservation of our sanctification is also by the Holy Spirit as we walk in obedience to his word.

> "Elect, according to the foreknowledge of God the Father, through sanctification of the Spirit, unto obedience and sprinkling of the blood of Jesus Christ: Grace unto you, and peace, be multiplied. Blessed be the God and Father of our Lord Jesus Christ, which according to his abundant mercy hath begotten us again unto a

lively hope by the resurrection of Jesus Christ from the dead, <u>to an inheritance incorruptible, and undefiled,</u> and that fadeth not away, reserved in heaven for you". (1Pe 1:2 to 4)

Also, we see in 1 Peter 1:2 through 4, that the inheritance that has been purchased for us by Yeshuah is incorruptible and undefiled. If we walk in the flesh, we will corrupt the inheritance and defile it so that the Godhead cannot indwell us to operate in and through us. Therefore to be able to operate the supernatural which Yashuah has promised, we must maintain our inheritance incorruptible and undefiled, then we will perform as Yashuah promised us. That also confirms the reason why we cannot access the Kingdom of God, because the Kingdom of God is not a physical geographic location but a spiritual location which is the temple of the believing saints of Yahweh. We must have the Holy Spirit fully operational in our lives, in order to legitimately work the work of the Kingdom, therefore we must wait upon the Holy Spirit to empower us for the work of the Kingdom. The Kingdom rulership is our inheritance according to Isa. 9:6, 7. Yashuah's birth gave us right to Sonship in Him and so as believers in resurrection power, we have become his body and His shoulders upon whom the government of the nations, rest for it is written "... and the government shall rest upon his shoulders". Therefore, according to Yashuah's word in John 14:20, "Yahweh in Christ and Christ in us and we in Christ, we have the Godhead dwelling in us and ruling through us in the earth. But the Godhead cannot rule in and through us without the Holy Spirit, so we must be in tune with the Holy Spirit in order to be in touch with the Godhead who will rule from within us. This is the reason believers are prophetic because Yashuah carries the Spirit of Prophesy and that should be our nature as well. "The testimony of Jesu Christ is the Spirit of Prophesy." (Rev. 19:10)

Therefore, all who are aspiring to manifest the joint heirship with Yashuah must press into Sonship first of all by being as Yashuah was, a faithful Son of Yahweh who walked in total obedience to His command and secure the right to the Kingdom. Yashuah has imparted to us the only way to receive the power to rule with Him. That power is within us. (Luke 17:21)

> "But, ye shall receive power after the Holy Spirit is come upon you: and ye shall be witnesses unto me, both in Jerusalem, and in all Judea, and in Samaria, and to the uttermost part of the earth". (Act 1:8)

Observe a difference here in Acts 1:8 about the work of the Holy Spirit and the work of the Holy Spirit that came upon the dust man when Elohim breathed into the dust man which Elohim called Adam. Both empower, but the empowerment in Acts. 1:8 was for Priestly functions

33

whereas in Gen 2:7, it was a creative life-giving power (Elohim) to make him a living soul.

The Holy Spirit is to the Godhead as breath is to the soul of man. Elohim the creator created man and breathed into man and man became a living soul. (Gen. 2:7)

> "And, El Olam formed man of the dust of the ground, and breathed into his nostrils the breath of life; and man became a living soul." (Gen 2:7)

This simply tells us that the Holy Spirit is the power of the Godhead and Yahweh's creation, especially for mankind. Man is the temple of Yahweh and in the end-time, man will become the Kingdom of Yahweh on earth according to Rev. 21:3 "Behold the Tabernacle of God is with men." The Holy Spirit operates in diverse ways and performs diverse operations.

> "And there are diversities of operations, but it is the same God who worketh all in all. But the manifestation of the Spirit is given to every man for profit' (1 Cor. 12:6, 7)

The breath (Ruach) of Elohim is the power and the Spirit of Elohim. Without the Ruach of Elohim man is as good as dead, and without the Holy Spirit (Ruach Ha Kodesh) imparting life into us, we would be just like robots and without His empowerment, we would be like dummies. That is the reason why Yahweh is drawing us back to himself through the Holy Ghost (Ruach Ha Kodesh). Yes, we recognize Yahweh the Father, and Yashuah God the Son, but we do not pay attention to Ruach Ha Kodesh, God the Holy Ghost who empowers and quickens us. As it is we are operating without the dominion that God planned for man to work with. Paul tells us in 1 Cor. 12 that all the gifts and workings of Yahweh was done by the self-same Spirit of Elohim. In other words, the Ruach is by Elohim operating in and through us for all mankind to profit withal. Furthermore, 1Cor. 12:8 thru 15 states that Saints of Yahweh are all endowed with these gifts and manifestations of the Ruach Ha Kodesh to operate through us as Yahweh's oracles and handimen here on earth for the world to benefit therefrom and bless the Most High (El Roi). The Saints have not only short changed themselves in this but they have robbed Yahweh of the glory due to Him. It is written, "Let your light so shine before men that they may see your good works, and glorify your Father in Heaven." These good works include the miracles and greater works that Yashuah promised we would do in his name and men shall be drawn unto Yahweh.

The Supernatural Work of the Holy Spirit (Ruach Ha Kodesh) in Kingdom building:

The Holy Ghost plays a major role in the Godhead to demonstrate and establish the power of Yahweh in creation and the building of the Kingdom of Yahweh in the earth. The Apostle Luke records saying "Neither shall they say, Lo, here! Or, lo there! For, behold, the kingdom of God is within you." (Luke 17:21) Here is the truth, the Kingdom of Yahweh is within us as individual believers. Therefore for any individual believer to show forth the glory and power of Yahweh, such individual must be filled with the Ruach of Elohim to an overflowing unto manifestation of the power of Elohim as shown to us by Yashuah while He was here on earth and now through the gifts of the Ruach Ha Kodesh enumerated in I Cor. 12. Therefore, Paul the Apostle admonishes us not to be ignorant of the gifts of the Holy Spirit because the gifts are the manifestation of the dynamos of Yahweh. Yashuah gave us the power and the glory before ascending to heaven. (Luke 10:19 and John 17:22) Yashuah left the power and the glory for us so we can manifest the Father to the world as He manifest Him to us. (John 17:5). We cannot fulfil Yashuah's command if we continue to negate the work of the Holy Ghost. This signifies that we are negating the very breath of Yahweh that will give life to our works and manifestation here on earth. The Godhead is complete within us His Saints waiting to be allowed to manifest Himself as we walk and work by the Holy Ghost. Therefore, we must renew our mind by the word and walk in the Spirit and avoid all carnal lust and its cravings that war against the Holy Spirit within us. Since the Kingdom of Yahweh is within us, we must let ourselves by led by Him for as many as are led by the Spirit of Yahweh are the sons of Yahweh.

We must understand the person and functions of the Holy Spirit in order to understand this book and make it effective for the transformation of our lives (both spiritual, physical, financial, mental and social). The reason why the church has been stagnant and seemingly dead since the last two millenniums is because she has neglected her power. Though she has embraced Yeshuah Hamashiach, she has left off the power and glory which He left for us to work with. She has not allowed the power of the Holy Spirit to operate in her activities and programs. We will deliberate more on the Person of the Holy Spirit in another chapter.

OBSERVATIONS AND VIEW POINTS

3.1 How would you discern the anointing in operation?

3.2 What importance does the Kingly anointing play in the church?

3.3 Is the Kingly anointing still functional today, since we are no longer under the monarchial rule? Give supporting scriptures.

3.4 What relevance has the kingly anointing in your personal life?

3.5 What part does the Holy Spirit play in the anointing?

3.6 What is the Hebrew name of the Holy Spirit?

3.7 What is the work of the Holy Spirit in the Church?

3.8 How would lack of humility hinder your access into the presence of Yahweh in your condition?

3.9 Assess your personal walk with God and see where you have been selfish or self-centered in relation with your walk with God in the past.

3.10 What is the importance of Isa. 9: 6, 7 and 2 Chr. 7:14? Give some examples of personal experience?

3.11 Is Acts. 1:8 vital for the work of the Kingdom of Yahweh in the earth?

3.12 What is the inheritance of the elect of Yahweh in the earth?

3.13 Where is the Kingdom of Yahweh at this moment?

3.14 In the Millenium, where will the Kingdom of Yahweh be? Give supporting Scripture.

CHAPTER 4

Accessing and Maintaining the Anointing

a.   Put on the Lord Yashuah and be Christ-like –
     Rom. 13:14.

We need to put on Christ and be renewed in our minds by putting on the mind of Christ through the logos, the written word. (Rom.12:1,2) As we walk in obedience to the logos, it becomes Rhema (lively word made flesh) in our lives. To the Jew the Torah is the Living Word, the word comes alive within them because they believe in the power of the God with the Torah. Even more so to the believer who walks in the Spirit, the word becomes flesh within us as we walk in obedience to the word. We need to think like Christ, walk like Christ, and talk like Christ for he is our King. We must imbibe his character in order to represent him perfectly, bearing in mind that He is coming for a glorious church without spots or wrinkles. (Col.3:10,12, Gal. 3:27, Eph. 5:27). The whole purpose of the anointing will be defeated if we do not imbibe his character and become perfect. That is why Yashuah told the Apostles to wait in Jerusalem until they receive the promse of the Father which will empower them to work the work of the Kingdom. It is one thing to access the anointing, it is yet another thing to maintain the anointing. The only way we can maintain the anointing is by walking in the Spirit. Paul warns us to walk in the Spirit so that we do not fulfill the lust of the flesh because the flesh lusts after the Spirit. (Gal. 5:16-17) When we walk in the Spirit, we are walking with the Godhead within us, but when we get into the flesh, we are out of touch with the Godhead. It is imperative to walk in the Spirit so as to maintain our anointing.

As we walk in the Spirit of the Godhead, we are walking in absolute communion with the Kingdom of Yahweh in the earth, and bringing the Kingdom of Yahweh into the earth. Walking in the Spirit of the Godhead, will lead to doing His will on earth as Yashuah taught us in the Lord's prayer. (Matt. 6:10) The Church who walks in the Spirit will become the perfect bride that Yashuah is preparing for his return. Those that walk in the Spirit are they that who are looking out for Yashuah's return. These are the company of the five wise virgins who had oil in their lamps when the Bridegroom came for the marriage supper. (Matt. 25:1,2) The Anointing is the sanctification of the believers. Anointing separates us from the others who have not the anointing just as we see in Matt. 25:8 – 10. The five foolish virgins could not make it into the bridal chamber, because by the time they returned, Yashuah told them out-right "Verily I say unto you, I know you not". The five wise virgins went in to the wedding that Yashuah is prepared. That is a type and shadow of the end-time Marriage Supper that Yashuah is preparing for His end-time bride espoused to Himself.

> "That he might present it to himself a glorious church, not having spot, or wrinkle, or any such thing; but that it should be holy and without blemish. "(Eph. 5:27)"

The Kingdom church is the bride of Yashuah Hamashiach. I specifically call the church "Kingdom Church" because there are religious churches that do not fit into the description of the bride of Christ. The bride of Yashuah will be without spot or wrinkle as she is described. Without spot or wrinkle means that she is without sin or leaven. She does not abuse the grace that Yashuah has paid the price for and permit herself to walk partly in the flesh and seasonally in the spirit. The Kingdom church comprises of believers who function under Rom. 8 verses 1, 2. These are believers who walk after the spirit and not after the flesh because we cannot access El Elyon in the flesh for God is Spirit and seeks those that worship him in Spirit and Truth. (John 4:24) We can only get the true direction from the mouth of El Elyon as we touch Him in the Spirit. Yashuah has commanded us to walk in the spirit so that we can be perfected and be adorned in our bridal garment in preparation of Yashuah's return. These believers are being transformed by the word, they do not conform to the world. (Rom. 12:1,2) They shall overcome the flesh and Spiritual wickedness in high places. Spiritual wickedness begins in our heart through rebellion and disobedience and graduates into the external demons that we have to, combat so as to regain the kingdom dominion that Satan stole from our Patriarch Adam. Yashuah is preparing his glorious Church (bride) without spot or wrinkle. We must put on the mind of Yashuah and take upon us his yoke and learn of Him for His yoke is easy and His burden light. Also, He declares that We must learn of Him from His meekness of Heart. (Matt. 11:29)

> "Let this mind be in you, which was also in Christ Jesus" Who, being in the form of God, thought it not robbery to be equal with God. But made Himself of no reputation, and took upon Him the form of a servant, and was made in the likeness of men." (Php 2:5 - 7)

Putting on the mind of Christ simply means that we his Saints should have his character and comport ourselves as He did while He was on earth. We are expected to demonstrate Christ-like life and make a difference on earth for the world to see and know that we are truly His disciples and not religious proclaimers who have no proof to show that we have known Christ at all. Putting on the mind and Character of Yashuah is the most important and thorough access into his Kingdom anointing, because we shall receive his Melchizedeck Anointing when we put on Christ the new man and take on his mind. We must be changed from within by putting on his mind and His righteousness as our outward garment. Christ-like transformation begins from within our inner man to the outward. The outward demonstration is the righteousness of Christ which the saints wear as a white linen garment that purity. Elohim said we must be holy unto Him for He the LORD our Yahweh is holy. And we must walk before Him and be perfect for He is perfect. Without holiness and righteousness which is the nature and character of Yashuah, we can neither access the anointing nor maintain it.

b. Humility:

> "And being found in fashion as a man, he humbled himself, and became obedient to death, even the death of the cross. Wherefore God also hath highly exalted him, and given him a name which is above other names." (Php. 2:8, 9)

Yashuah Hamashiach our Master who is also our standard/mirror honors the word and submits himself to the word. We also must submit ourselves to the word, because the Holy Spirit resists the proud but gives grace to the humble. In verse 9, we see that Elohim highly exalted Yashuah for humbling himself. Humility is a facilitator to the anointing. We make a way for the Holy Spirit to feel comfortable within us and operate through us if we humble ourselves. But when we deny Him expression through us because, we run ahead of him and do as we please, we grieve Him and he departs from us. It is a pathetic state for one who was once walking in the Spirit to suddenly start walking in the flesh. Paul calls such ones "Foolish Galatians". Yahweh likes to lead us through his Holy Spirit. David the psalmist says in Psalm 48:14. "For, this Elyon is our Elohim, He will be our *guide* from now, even unto the end". Nothing that we have that did not come from Him. All that we have came from Him and we are bound to reverence Him if we want to continue under His anointing. John the Baptist prayed that Yashuah will increase while he decreases, this is pertinent because we cannot have two captains in one boat. Therefore, we cannot steer the boat while Yashuah is also steering the boat of our lives. Humility releases the Holy Spirit to take absolute control in establishing the will of Yahweh.

c. Selflessness or Self-centeredness

The principle for our salvation and redemption is LOVE for the World. For God so loved the world that He gave his only begotten son, that whosoever believeth in him should not perish but have everlasting life. (John 3:16) The same love prompted Yashuah to bear the cross of death all the way and did not give up. He came to show the way and there is no short cut to the anointing. We have to love like Yashuah loved us, and not be selfish. We must give up ourselves or deny ourselves, carry our cross and follow Yashuah watching our lives lest we defile our priesthood by any means. The Priestly sanctification is very vital and any wrong character will defile the priest and become as leaven in the temple. It is written that a little leaven leaveneth the whole lump. (1 Cor.5:6) End time Priests aspiring for the holy anointing must be generous and compassionate. They must treat others as they desire to be treated. (Luke 6:31) In the end we will be like these ones recorded in Rev. 14:4.

> "These are they which were not defiled with women; for they are virgins. These are they which follow the Lamb whithersoever He goeth. These were redeemed from among men, being the first fruits unto God and to the Lamb". (Rev 14:4)

Amongst this company of martyrs, was Stephen, in Acts. 7:60. Stephen the martyr not only gave up his life to be stoned to death without resistance, but he knelt down and prayed to Yashuah Hamashiach to forgive those who stoned him and not lay the sin at their charge. (Acts. 7:60). This is the heart of those who aspire towards the Holy Spirit End Time Kingdom Anointing.

The good thing about all this is that we do not have to do this personally, all we need to do is set our hearts in a position of willingness and obedience and the Holy Spirit Himself will equip us and draw us into His presence. It is as it were like Esther who set her mind to go in unto King Ahasuerus. She waited upon God for access through praying and fasting for three days, and on the third day, King Ahazuerus stretched the golden scepter to give her <u>access into the presence of the King.</u> She set her mind to go speak with the King in behalf of her brethren, so she told her uncle Mordecai to gather the Jews together and fast along with her for three days and at the end she risked her life and went in unto the King.

> "Go, gather together all the Jews that are present in Shushan, and fast ye for me, and neither eat nor drink three days, night or day: I also and my maidens will fast likewise and so will I go in unto the king, which is not according to the law: <u>and if I perish, I</u> <u>perish</u>." Now it came to pass on the third day, that Esther put on her royal apparel, and stood in the inner court of the king's house, over against the king's house: and the king sat upon his royal throne in the royal house, over against the gate of the house". (Esth. 5:1-3. Esth. 4:16)

> "And it was so, when the king saw Esther the queen standing in the court, that she obtained favour in his sight: and

the king held out to Esther the golden
sceptre that *was* in his hand. So, Esther
drew near, and touched the top of the
sceptre. Then said the king unto her,
What wilt thou, queen Esther? and what
is thy request? it shall be even given thee
to the half of the kingdom." (Est 5:2 -3)

Note the selflessness of Queen Esther in chapter 4:16
(… if I perish I perish"), and how Yahweh granted her
favour because she did not consider her life, she put her
life in jeopardy for the lives of the Jews in Shushan the
Palace. Yashuah also gave up his life for us. And got us
the victory by His preceious blood. So, He expects us also
to give up our lives for the sake of our brethren. Yashuah
sanctified himself for our sakes and we also must sanctify
ourselves for the sake of the bride. (John 17:19) As we
give up ourselves for the church and pray and intercede,
Yashuah will work through us to perform His miracles
in and through us for the world to see and glorify our
Elohim in heaven and will also exalt us and grant us the
anointing we need to dwell in His presence.

So, we see that Yahweh highly exalted Yeshuah
because He was obedient and humble. Yahweh exalts
the humble but abases the proud. As King Ahasuerus
favored Esther and granted her half of his kingdom, so
shall Yahweh grant us favor and access into the Kingdom
of God. He will anoint us, if we are willing to walk in

His ways. Yeshuah showed us the example, it is now left to us to take up the challenge and possess our dominion.

    d.   Confidence and Assurance in the name of Yashuah.

We must have that total confidence and assurance that there is power in the name of Yashuah for He is the word of God and at the mention of His name every knee bows and every knee confesses that Yashuah is Lord. The Kingdom of God is a mystery, and without absolute working faith, we cannot venture to access it. It is a path only for the foolish and the helpless who has no hope in any other but Yashuah. It is a place where you will be met with incredible situations and beauty that we have never beheld. When God starts revealing the Kingdom to us, we must be able to identify with Him in it all. Yahweh is a mighty God (Jehovah), His ways are unsearchable, no man can know it. Our hearts must be so renewed and transformed that we can conform to His word and the mystery thereof. I am talking about expecting some miraculous reality in our lives and through us!!!!!! When these Mysteries happen, no-one can ever imagine, people will stand in awe and amazement. This is the express work of the Kingdom Anointing upon the vessels of Yahweh.

> "That, at the mention of the name
> of Yeshuah, every knee should bow, of
> things in heaven, and things on earth,

and things under the earth. And that
every tongue should confess that Jesus
Christ is Lord, to the glory of God the
Father. Wherefore, my beloved, as
ye have always obeyed, not as in my
presence only, but now much more in
my absence, work out your own salvation
with fear and trembling. For, it is God
who worketh in you both to will and to
do of his good pleasure." (Php 2:10 – 13)

Beloved, God is calling us to total submission to his
word. We have departed from his word in diverse ways,
and He is calling us to return to divine order. We have
been operating under Democracy, but the LORD had
ordained his people to walk under Theocracy according
to Isa. 9:6 -7.

"For to us a child is born, unto us a
son is given:" This part of the scripture
has been fulfilled by Jesus Christ birth
and ministry as a son. As a son He has
shown us how to follow in his step to
secure the kingdom. (Isa 9:6a) Yashuah
has laid the foundation, and now we
are to build upon it the same quality of
spiritual fruits and bricks as He laid."

"… and the government shall be upon his shoulder:
and his name shall be called Wonderful, Counselor, The

mighty God, The everlasting Father, The Prince of Peace". (Isa, 9:6b) We are the body of Yashuah Hamashiach. The body bears the shoulder, therefore without gain-saying, we understand that the government of the nations is upon the Saints of Yashuah. We are the governors of the nations, but we can only govern through his Holy Spirit guidance according to the pattern He gives us. As my head is to my body, so is Christ head to us his body. We must get the unction and the anointing from Him. This is what this book is all about.

> "Of the increase of his government and peace there shall be no end, upon the throne of David, and upon his kingdom, to order it, and to establish it with judgment and with justice from henceforth even for-ever. The zeal of the LORD of hosts will perform this". (Isa 9:7)

Yashuah laid this foundation of the body by his blood and commanded us to be ruler over the nations of the world through the authority He has achieved. The ruling of the nations will be ordered by Yahweh as we receive instructions from the Holy Spirit to speak to the nations. This governmental power operating through the body of Yashuah by the Holy Spirit is the theocratic government of God. As it is prophesied by the prophet, "And the LORD shall be King over all the earth; in that day, there shall be one LORD and His name one." (Zech. 14:9) The LORD shall rule in and through us until He descends, the Godhead descends in Rev. 22:1,2 to rule eternally.

Halleluya!!! All that the church needs for growth and establishment is embedded in Yashuah and He gave us the glory to continue the work, (John 17:22). We must stop showing forth the form of Godliness but denying the power thereof and look unto Yashuah the author and finisher of all things to perfect what He has started. (II Tim. 3:5). We the Saints of Yahweh have the power, the wisdom and insight that is needed to rule the world. We are the people who will judge the world. (1 Cor. 6:2) We will judge the world and speak as He directs and the world will have to listen. As we allow Him to speak and act through us we are occupying the ruling position that He told us to occupy till He comes.

Yashuah is not a task master who tells us to do something without making adequate provision. He has told us that if we believe in Him, we will do the works that He did and even greater works shall we do. (John 14:12). He made this provision available to all believers in preparation for a time that will come for the remnant of the Church who is adorned as a bride prepared for her groom will emerge to rule with Him on earth with Him. The Lord is going to govern the church, and the whole earth which He created, for the earth must be filled with the knowledge of the glory of God even as the waters cover the sea, then the Lord will appear to take over the rulership. (Hab. 2:14). This is the reason He said, his people must pray so that He will heal our land (2 Chr. 7:14.).

> "If my people, who are called by
> my name, shall humble themselves, and
> pray, and seek my face, and turn from
> their wicked ways; then will I hear from
> heaven, and will forgive their sin, and
> will heal their land". (2Ch 7:14)

Testimonies of Answered Prayers:

In 2011, the Yahweh Global Personal Prophetic Intercessory group prayed prophetically as the LORD commanded for the tyrannic presidency of Mubarak over Egypt to cease. Shortly after we prayed, The President, Hoseni Mubarak, who ruled over Egypt for thirty years, resigned his position on February. 11, 2011.

We also prayed during the same period for Libya and in October, the tyrannic revolutionist, President who forcibly took over rulership and ruled over Libya for forty-two years was ousted, and killed in the battle of Sirte.

In 2012, The Yahweh Global Personal Prophetic and Intercessory group prayed as the LORD directed. Our Chief Cornerstone Yashuah Hamashiach, the heavenly Intercessor had directed us to pray that He should reveal himself in visions and dreams, to the muslims so that they will turn over to Him. Reports came to us at a meeting of Benny Hinn that 11,500 muslims dreamed seeing Yashuah and became converted overnight.

The prophesy in Isa. 9:6,7 "….. and the government shall be upon his shoulders … And of the increase and peace thereof, there shall be no end". This prophecy by Isa. 9:6, 7 is fulfilled as we, the body of Christ rise up to pray and intercede as He commands.

There are so many testimonies that we cannot enumerate, and much more that we have not heard about. This anointing to rule in Christ's behalf, does not come cheaply, it demands our total commitment and dedication to the LORD and as we sit before him.

Yahweh is calling on His people to judge wickedness in the land so that He will heal the land. SO I USE THIS MEANS AND OPPORTUNITY TO CALL ON INTERCESSORS, PERSONAL PROPHETIC INTERCESSORS OF YAHWEH, TO HEED YAHWEH'S HEART CRY AND ARISE, HUMBLE OURSELVES, FORSAKE OUR OWN WICKED WAYS AND SEEK HIS FACE. HE HAS PROMISED, AND HE WILL HEAL BECAUSE HE IS A COVENANT KEEPER. IF WE REGARD SIN IN OUR HEARTS, HE WILL NOT HEAR US. THE INSTRUCTION IS "HUMBLE THEMSELVES, PRAY AND SEEK MY FACE, AND TURN FROM THEIR WICKED WAYS".: We cannot pray unto Yahweh with sin in our hearts. He is too holy to behold iniquity, therefore before we come into His presence, we must sanctify ourselves, and forsake our sins, because Yahweh is able to discern all hypocricies in our hearts. We cannot mock Him. It is written, "If My people, which are called by My name, shall humble themselves, and pray, and seek My face, and turn from their wicked ways; then will I hear from heaven, and will forgive their sin, and will heal their land". (2 Chr. 7:14)

e.   Discerning the entrance of the anointing:

As we sit before the Lord either worshiping and praying, in communion with him whether individually or corporately, we must be conscious of his presence, when He moves in, if we are not, He will pass on and it might take us another 30 minutes or perhaps another time before we get Him again. We have to be very sensitive to his presence and constrain him once we catch him. Sometimes, He loves a particular song or worship and wants us to linger on until He expresses Himself or reveals Himself to us and give us a direction to follow. Once we key into the Spirit of the anointing, we must ensure that we follow on attentively and maintain our spiritual stand or else we lose Him by stepping away in the flesh.

Diverse persons experience His presence in divers ways. Sometimes we feel some shrills all over our body, sometimes, it could be in one particular part of the body, like me, it begins with my right hand, or sometimes, he comes as fire and we feel the warmth of His presence etc. Sometimes, He just appears in a vision and we feel the weight of the glory of His presence.

f.   Maintaining and constraining the Anointing:

"And grieve not the Holy Spirit of
God, whereby ye are sealed unto the day
of redemption. Let all bitterness, and
wrath, and anger, and clamour, and evil

> speaking, be put away from you, with all
> malice. And be ye kind one to another,
> tenderhearted, forgiving one another,
> even as Yahweh hath forgiven you". (Eph
> 4:30 – 32)

Carnality, bitterness, malice and all manners of un-holy characters within us will grieve the Holy Spirit. Lack of discernment will also grieve the Holy Spirit and cause him to withdraw.

It is one thing to get the anointing, it is yet another thing to maintain and constrain the anointing to remain with you. There are many ministers of Yahweh today who began well with the anointing, but have departed from the anointing and have become Ichabod. "Gal. 3:1,2 says, "O ye foolish Galatians, who hath bewitched you that ye should not obey the Truth, before whose eyes Yeshuah Hamashiach hath been evidently set forth, crucified among you? Received ye the Holy Spirit by law or by hearing of faith?" It is important to persist in Faith and in the Holy Spirit. If we stray into the flesh or unbelief as we move on, we will grieve the Holy Spirit and the anointing will quit on us. The law is of the flesh and anything flesh is not in the Divine realm of Yahweh and cannot stand before His Holy presence. Therefore, Paul the Apostle steadfastly warns us to "walk in the Spirit that we may not fulfill the lust of the flesh." Yashuah also said that He will build His church and the gates of hell shall not prevail against it.

I can testify to this. In my Church in California, I

was one of the personal intercessors for my Pastor. One day as I was interceding for her, the Lord gave me an open-eye vision of her sitting on the left lap of Jehovah God; she was dressed in a white bridal garment, with golden shoes on her feet and a crown on her head. The Lord had his left hand around her shoulders, and with his right hand He was giving her instructions. And I heard the LORD say to me "This is my daughter and she takes the word from my mouth and gives to my people. She is spiritual and there must be no flesh around her." I understood what He said because I was only about three months new in her church then and I needed to know the constitution there as a member of the intercessory group, that was part of my orientation. I wanted to speak to her personally and I said something carnal and I saw her shrink and looked at me in disapproval and walked away. I understood her action very well as saying, No, don't draw me out of the anointing, then I remembered what the Lord told me in the vision. On another occasion, she was ministering at the pulpit and the Lord showed me the face of the Lion of the tribe of Judah in the center of the pulpit, and water was gushing out of the mouth of the Lion and many people were rushing to drink from the Lion's mouth. I asked the LORD what that vision meant and He said that she was speaking as the oracle of Yashuah Hamashiach. He said she was speaking directly from the Spirit of Yashuah, the Lion of the Tribe of Judah and people were rushing to drink from his mouth.

A biblical example of that is Peter telling Yashuah not to go to Jerusalem, Yashuah rebuked him and told him that he savours not the things of the spirit but of the flesh (Matt. 16:23). Therefore, it is vital that we not only covet the anointing, but we must also constrain and restraint the anointing once we get Him.

OBSERVATIONS AND VIEW POINTS

1. a. How do we put on Christ mind?
   b. Why should we put on the Mind of Christ? Illustrate an example.

2. a. What is Humility? Give examples of those who walked in Humility besides Yeshuah.
   b. Why did Paul call the Galatians "Foolish"? Support your answer with any person you
   c. Give examples of some foolish Galatians that you know who are like that.
   d. How can we help such persons to move in the Spirit?

3. a. What is the foundation of our Salvation?
   b. How are we expected to build upon that Foundation?
   c. What did Yashuah command us to do in order to follow him? Cite scripture.
   d. Give examples of person you know that walked as Rev. 14:4 says.
   e. Briefly narrate the walk of anyone you know that can be described with Rev. 14:4.

f. Give an example and the scripture of someone who demonstrated a selfless character and was ready to give her life for the sake of others in the Hebrew Scriptures (OT).

g. What did she do?

h. Give some pre-requisites of how one can access the Kingdom Anointing?

i. By whose power and direction can we enter in?

j. What part of the scripture in Isa. 9;6 and 7, has been fulfilled and by who?

k. What part is yet to be fulfilled and by who?

l. What will be done to fulfill the later part? Quote the scripture.

m. What is the spiritual responsibility of the people of God to bring this to pass? Cite the scripture.

n. Give one or two Testimonies of your Prayers that have been answered.

o. What is your plan to access the Kingdom Anointing in order to activate the power of the Kingdom of God within you?

CHAPTER 5

Access Into Open Heaven

a. Fear and reverence to God:

Perceiving the presence of Yahweh is the most awesome thing that can happen to a believer.

> "And He said, I beseech thee, shew me thy glory.
> And he said, I will make all My goodness pass before thee, and I will proclaim the name of the LORD before thee; and will be gracious to whom I will be gracious, and will shew mercy on whom I will shew mercy. And he said; Thou canst not see my face: for there shall no man see me, and live." (Exo 33:18, 20)

Moses requested to see Yahweh's face (glory) and God said he could not see his face rather He will show him the glory of His backside. So, if Yahweh's backside was so glorious, how much more his face. Therefore, we must fear and reverence Yahweh. When Moses finally stood before Yahweh on Mount Sinai for forty days and forty nights, by the time Moses came down, his face was so radiant and glowing that the people could not look at him, he had to put a veil over his face, before the children of Israel could look on his face. Exo. 34:27 – 30. That is what the glory of the LORD does to anyone that accesses his presence. There is a transformation that takes place both in the person's character and appearance. One thing we must note here is the fact that when we see Yahweh's face, our natural humanity dies but the Spirit is transformed to conform with the nature of Yahweh within us. So now let us see how to enter into his presence.

Yahweh told Moses to tell the people what they needed to do in Deut. 10: 12 – 20.

> "And now Israel, what doth the LORD
> thy God require of thee, but to fear the
> LORD thy God, to walk in all his ways
> and to love him, and to serve the LORD
> thy God with all thy heart and with all
> thy soul." (Deut. 10:12).

Only the LORD had delight in thy fathers to love them, and he chose their seed after them, even you, above all people, as it is this day. (Deut. 10:15)

A pre-requisite is the fear of Yahweh, He desires

and deserves our reverential fear and trust because that is the beginning of wisdom. Yahweh is worthy of all reverence. In a place of reverence, true worship sets in, and pure fellowship with Yahweh arises. And it is in a time of worship in Spirit and intimate worship with God that the anointing is built up and Yahweh is so pleased that He just pours out His anointing upon us and we feel his supernatural presence rising up within our Spirit. When we experience the joy of being in sweet fellowship with Yahweh, His presence flows over us in such a tremendous way that we get drawn into the depth of his love and we are lost in ecstasy.

b. Circumcision of our Hearts:

"Circumcise therefore the foreskin of
your heart, and be no more stiff-necked.
For the LORD your God is God of gods,
and LORD of lords, a great God, a mighty,
and a terrible, who regards not persons,
nor takes reward:" (Deut. 10:16, 17)

Circumcision of hearts means a total separation from all carnality and fleshly lusts. No carnal Christian can ascend the spiritual height of Yahweh's glory as the psalmist says in Psalm 1:1-3. We must put away all our carnal thoughts and desires and allow our Spirit to rise and grasp the mind of Yahweh. Then his word will be meaningful to us. El Elyon is Spirit and they that worship him must worship him in Spirit and Truth. The anointing is attained from worship in the Spirit because when we worship in the spirit, we are lifted up from the earth realm and we touch Yahweh with our Spirit at the place of the Altar of incense right before the Mercy Seat where He said He will meet with us, and a union is formed. Once a union is formed, we become one with the Lord and an intimate relationship brings about a bridal chamber experience and fruitfulness. There is an impartation taking place at that time, this experience is a manifestation of John 14:21.

As we worship in the Spirit and have spiritual fellowship with the LORD, the heavens over us are opened and we have access into His very presence. In the presence of the LORD, we feel nothing but love, peace and such serenity that we cannot feel anything but love towards others because that is Yahweh's nature and everything or everyone that comes in contact with Him exhibits the same attribute. He gives everyone alike judgment and mercy wherever necessary.

> "He executes the judgment of the fatherless and widow, and loves the stranger, in giving him food and raiment. Love ye therefore the stranger: for ye were strangers in the land of Egypt. Thou shalt fear the LORD thy Elyon; Him shalt thou serve, and to Him shalt thou cleave, and swear by his name". (Deut. 10:18- 20)

It is Yahweh's commandment that we love the stranger for then we really show the nature of Yahweh in us, for Yahweh is love and he that loves is born of Yahweh. (John 4:7).

Love is a very vital pre-requisite to the Kingdom anointing because the foundation of the kingdom is love: "For God so loved the world that He gave his only begotten son that whosoever believeth in him should not perish but have everlasting life." (John 3:16) Furthermore, Jesus said in John 14:15 that if we love him, we should keep his commandment. Yeshuah answered and said unto him, "If a man love me, he will keep my words: and my Father will love him, and we will come unto him, and make our abode with him." (Joh 14:23). This is the crux of the whole issue of the Kingdom. "LOVE" Without Love we cannot keep the commandment, and if we do not keep the commandment of Yahweh, we will have no part in Yeshuah and the Godhead. So, love is the foundation, and we must build love on it and finish it in the Kingdom in love.

"The same came to Jesus by night, and said to him, Rabbi, we know that thou art a teacher come from God; for, no man can do these miracles that thou doest, except God be with him. Jesus answered and said to him, Verily, verily, I say to thee; Except a man be born again,

> he cannot see the kingdom of God.
> Nicodemus says to him; How can a man
> be born again when he is old, can he
> enter the second time into his mother's
> womb, and be born? Jesus answered,
> Verily, verily, I say to thee; Except a man
> be born of water, and of the Spirit, he
> cannot enter into the kingdom of God.
> That which is born of the flesh, is flesh;
> and that which is born of the Spirit, is
> Spirit". (John 3:2 – 6)

The Love of Yashuah constraints us to obey His commandment to be born again. In order to move onto perfection through the Holy Spirit, we must continue in obedience to His further commandment. That is what Nicodemus learned and we must also learn and obey. First pre-requisite is to be born again, by believing in Yeshuah and receiving him into our hearts and that is the only way into the Kingdom.

> "Marvel not that I said to thee, Ye
> must be born again. The wind blows
> where it will, and thou hearest the sound
> of it, but canst not tell whence it cometh,
> and whither it goes: so is every one that is
> born of the Spirit. Nicodemus answered
> and said to him, "How can these things
> be? Jesus answered and said to him". Art
> thou a teacher of Israel, and knows not

these things? Verily, verily, I say to thee, We speak what we know, and testify what we have seen; and ye receive not our testimony. If I have told you earthly things, and ye believe not, how will ye believe if I tell you heavenly things? And no man hath ascended to heaven, but He that came down from heaven, even the Son of man who is in heaven. And as Moses lifted up the serpent in the wilderness, even so must the Son of man be lifted up: That whoever believeth in Him should not perish, but have eternal life. For God so loved the world, that he gave his only-begotten Son, that whoever believeth in him, should not perish, but have everlasting life. For God sent not his Son into the world to condemn the world, but that the world through him may be saved". (John 3:7 -17)

Nicodemus has been a Torah teacher in the Synagogue. The Living Torah is all about Yashuah therefore He asked Nicodemus why he did not understand that he must be born again (Spiritually) in order to enter the Kingdom of Yahweh. The Lamb that was slain and the blood smeered on the door-post was a type and shadow of Yashuah who was slain at Calvary for the redemption of mankind. All that is born of flesh is flesh, but he that receives the Lord Yashuah is being born of the Spirit. Unfortunately,

Nicodemus or anyone in the flesh cannot understand spiritual matters because the word of Yahweh is spiritually discerned. The believers of the 21st century church are in the same condition, because they find it difficult to walk in the Spirit as Paul said "Walk ye in the Spirit that ye may not fulfill the lust of the flesh. (Gal. 5:16). The carnally minded cannot understand spiritual matters. So imagine what will happen, if we cannot understand the bible, how can we understand Spiritual matters and have access to the Kingdom of Yahweh or even approach to the divine nature and consuming presence of Yahweh. We must worship Yahweh in Spirit and Truth so that we can work the work of Yashuah Hamashiach as He also showed us an example to follow Him in the same way.

> "That God anointed Jesus of Nazareth
> with the Holy Spirit and with power:
> who went about doing good, and healing
> all that were oppressed by the devil; for
> God was with him". (Acts 10:38)

This anointing by which Yahweh anointed Yashuah flows to us as we worship in Spirit and in Truth. As disciples of Yashuah, we must follow Him in the same way being sensitive and yielded to the control and direction of the Holy Spirit. Then we will be able to do the works that Yashuah worked and even greater work.

In Deut. 10, the LORD told Moses, what they needed to do:

1. "To Love the LORD, For the Father loveth the Son, and showeth him all things that himself doeth: and he will show him greater works than these, that ye may marvel." In obedience and example to us, Yeshuah also said" I can of my own self do nothing: as I hear, I judge: and my judgment is just; because I seek not my own will, but the will of the Father who hath sent me." (John 5: 20, 30)

Yeshuah Hamashiach is obedient to the core keeping the words that were prophesied by Moses because they are Yahweh's word. Therefore, in continuation He ensures that He does not do anything which the Father has not commanded either by vision, revelation or by the logos. In like manner, we His followers are expected to emulated Him as He has written. The Holy Spirit was sent to empower us to work in obedience as well as operate the gifts that are necessary for the fulfilment of the word of the Kingdom. Therefore, we must realize that we cannot access the Kingdom of Yahweh in our flesh. For it is not by power, not by might, but by my Spirit saith the LORD Hashem.

Furthermore, the foundation of our Salvation and Redemption is LOVE. The access to the Kingdom will be revealed to all who LOVE THE LORD, just like a father who reveals all his wealth to his best son and nothing is hid from him. Jesus was so pleased with John the divine that He revealed Himself and his Kingdom to him in diverse ways. (Rev. 1:1, 2)

2. "To fear the LORD: It is written that the FEAR of the LORD is the beginning of wisdom."

This means that we must revere the LORD. The church has derailed from Yahweh's pattern because there is no fear and no reverence of Hashem anymore in the heart of the people. Everyone does his own will according to the Prophet Isaiah.

> "Wherefore have we fasted, *say they,* and thou seest not? *wherefore* have we afflicted our soul, and thou takest no knowledge? Behold, in the day of your fast ye find pleasure, and exact all your labours". (Isa. 58:3)

3. "Keeping the Sabbath holy. "If thou turn away thy foot from the Sabbath, *from* doing thy pleasure on my holy day; and call the Sabbath a delight, the holy of the LORD, honourable; and shalt honour him, not doing thine own ways, nor finding thine own pleasure, nor speaking *thine own* words. Then shalt thou delight

thyself in the LORD; and I will cause thee
to ride upon the high places of the earth,
and feed thee with the heritage of Jacob
thy father: for the mouth of the LORD
hath spoken it". (Isa 58:13, 14)

**The Sabbath of the LORD is a day of rest which
he commanded us to honor. The rest of the LORD is
for us to walk strictly by his spirit and not walk in
our own ways. He is King of kings and Lord of lords.
He must be obeyed by his subjects. The Kingdom of
Yahweh cannot be filled with rebellious children
that walk contrary to the rules of the Kingdom just
like King Saul did and was rejected. We must have
an understanding of the Rest of Yahweh, it is not
depicted by the number of days in a week. Yahweh
rested from His work of creation after He formed
man and breathed on him on the sixth day. He ceased
from working and entered into a rest from creation.
So Yahweh also expect us to cease from our labour of
working and enter into His rest.**

"Let us therefore fear, lest, a promise
being left us of entering into his rest, any
of you should seem to come short of
it. For unto us was the gospel preached,
as well as unto them: but the word
preached did not profit them, not being
mixed with faith in them that heard
it. For we which have believed do enter

> into rest, as he said, As I have sworn in
> my wrath, if they shall enter into my
> rest: although the works were finished
> from the foundation of the world. For
> he spake in a certain place of the seventh
> day on this wise, And God did rest the
> seventh day from all his works." (Heb
> 4:1-4)

All believers must cease from their works and do the works of Yahweh as Yashuah commanded. The church has gone so deep into religious worship that the Holy Spirit has been left out of the activities of most services unto Yahweh. Nevertheless, the remnant are beginning to understand this fact and are striving to be sensitive to the Holy Spirit leading so they can cease from their own works and work the work of Yahweh according to divine order.

Another aspect of the wrong understanding of the Sabbath is the day of worship chosen by the 21st century believers. The 21st century church has been diverted and perverted from the true Sabbath prescribed by Yahweh and have rather chosen a day according to the Gregorian calender to worship Yahweh because they do not know the Hebrew calendar. The Gregorian calendar has the first day of the week being Monday and Sunday as the seventh day, whereas according to the Hebrew calendar, Sunday is the first day of the week which gives us Saturday as the seventh day.

Therefore, the real Sabbath day of worship is supposed to be Saturday.

> "And to make thee high above all nations which he hath made, in praise, and in name, and in honour; and that thou mayest be an holy people unto the LORD thy God, as he hath spoken." (Deu 26:19)

The high places referred to here is the spiritual realm which you and I will inherit as we consecrate ourselves to him. We shall be the kings in His kingdom on earth while He assumes His place as the King of kings and He will rule and reign in and through us according to John 14:20, 21.

c.   Circumcision the foreskins of the flesh.

This circumcision is not a natural circumcision but a spiritual one which Yeshuah refers to in John 3: 5 as being baptized in water and the spirit. Yeshuah stated very clearly that we can see the kingdom, if we are baptized in water. But in verse 5, Jesus specified, that "Verily, verily; Except a man be born of water and of the spirit, he cannot **enter** the Kingdom of GOD.

What does it mean to be baptized of the spirit? Being born of the Spirit means that the Holy Spirit comes upon us as it did in Acts 2:1. It is generally accompanied with an evidence of speaking in the tongues. Baptism in the

Holy Spirit is a vital pre-requisite for believers because when we are filled with the Holy Spirit, we will be able to communicate with the Godhead in His own language so we are edified. This experience is called the circumcision of our hearts, because when the spirit comes upon us, our hearts are transformed from the worldly condition to a divine condition. When our hearts are transformed, we cannot conform to the world anymore. We will desire to be renewed daily by the word, so that the Kingdom of God will be revealed unto us more and more until the word becomes a mirror to us and we can see our own lives when we read the bible. When our lives are transformed into the image and likeness of Yashuah, we can abide continually in the presence of the Most-High. (John 15:3-5)

It is only at this point that we can hear the voice of our master in diverse ways, either audibly, or by revelation and other ways peculiar to each individual.

Yeshuah expects us to be able to hear him not only through the word, but through other ways, so that he can lead us. How else can we obey Him if we do not hear Him speaking to us. He communicates with us audibly or by impression upon our heart or through signs, and dreams and visions. The LORD GOD wants to be the author and finisher of our lives. We cannot live with someone that we do not hear or discuss with. We cannot even obey Him if our hearts are not converted to him.

We believers need to determine to obey the Savior now and ask him to circumcise our hearts afresh, and baptize us by his spirit in order to unite us with him and the Godhead. God is Spirit and they that worship Him must worship Him in Spirit and in truth.

The only access into the Kingdom of God is by the spirit, for God is spirit and He desires those that worship Him to worship Him in spirit and in truth. There is an anointing that breaks all bondages when we step into the spirit. This anointing does a peculiar work in us that we do not understand, until we see the manifestation.

Desire him now, and He shall come unto you in Jesus name.

d.   Appropriate Priestly Garment:

The dressing of the Priest entering into Yahweh's presence is very vital. Queen Esther entered into the King's court in her full queenly regalia. Yahweh has also commanded a proper Priestly Garment for the Priest. He told Moses to make Holy Garments according to His specification to clothe Aaron and his sons for service before Him in the Priest's office.

Though the 21st century priests are not demanded to wear this specially tailored garment, but every piece of the priestly garment has a relevant spiritual meaning. For instance, the white linen of the priest's garment stands for "honesty and purity". The garment itself stands for righteousness. The Mitre stands for Helmet of Salvation. The girdle stands for the act of readiness for priestly work. (Exo. 28:1,2)

The Garments of the High Priest

Defining the relevance of the Priestly
Garment in the New Testament – Exo. 28

The Priest's garment in Hebrew has relevant meaning to the quality and expected duties of the New Testament Priests. The New Testament Priests garment denotes the characerics, lifestyle, and sanctification relevant to the position and duty of the Priests. Although the New Testament Priests do not have to dress up in the full regalia that Hashem commanded Moses, to have made by specially anointed craftsman, they are expected to comport their lives in accordance to what the various parts of the garment replicates. (Exo. 28:3)

Garment Piece	Materials and Description	Old Testament Relevance	New Testament Relevance
Mitre (Turban) Helmet of Salvation (Eph. 6:17)	Fine Linen	Atone for Pride of Countenance (Ps.10:4)	Covering of Savior Head of the church
Golden Emblem bearing "Holiness unto YHVH"	Gold Plate worn on the forehead of the Priest	Atonement for arrogance and pride	Gold plate means purity of mind demonstrating Holiness unto Yahweh

Onyx Stone, each stone with six names of the 12 tribes of Israel.		The twelve tribes of Israel are scattered all over the world and we are the offspring of the twelve tribes.	Yashuah is the lively stone. This chief corner stone rejected by man. Two is the number of witness, six is Man, twelve is number of government. The government is upon the shoulder of Yashuah. We are bearing the shoulders of Yashuah.
Breastplate of Judgement (Exo. 28:17 – 21)	The breastplate is made with stones in 12 different compartments. (Exo.28:21)	Amongst the stones were two names Hurim and Thummim that signal approval or non-approval of Yahweh for a problem. Aaron shall bear the names of the children on his heart. (Exo.28:30)	Breastplate of Righteousness. The righteousness of the Saints will judge the world, (Eph. 6:14) Our Saviour and Chief intercessor bears our names upon his heart for ever interceding for us. We are joint heirs with and co-intercessors.
Binding the Breastplate with rings.	Two Rings	To keep the breastplate in place.	Rings symbolize the marriage bond between the Yashuah and His Church, So that the saints are united with Yashuah because our righteousness is in Him.

Girdle Exo. 28:27	A sash	Symbolizes Ever-ready Soldier of Yahweh, and.	Girdle of Truth for the loins. (Eph. 6:17) Symbolizes the Word of Truth and the Person of Truth. Humility – Character of being willing to serve. Yeshuah washing the *Talmidim's* feet (John 13: 4-10). He is the Golden Girdle in Rev. 1:13.
Ephod	Embroidered with blue, purple, scarlet and gold, (heavenly glory) (Exo. 28:6)	Atone for idolatory.	The intricate embroidery symbolizes the inter-mingling of the body of Yashuah with Him in character and at the place of worship. (John 14:23) It also symbolizes the heavenly glory of the Godhead abiding with the saints here in the planet earth. (Rev. 11:15, 21:1-3)
Robe of the Ephod	Made of blue.	*Atonement for evil speech.* (*Techelet*) (Col. 3:8)	The Ephod is worn over the robe. Robe of atonement. Yashuah is our atonement, bears our sins upon his body, and the ephod covers us for eternal security. We also have to put off our old nature that is corrupt with flesh and put on the new man and cleave to Him. Col. 3:9, 10)

Golden Bell/ Pomegranates		The priest's robe is made with golden bells and pomegranate at the helm. The golden bells ring to announce danger if the priest sins against Hashem in the Holy of Holies and he is struck down he is dragged out with a rope that is attached to the robe. The Pomegranates represent fruitfulness of the work of the priest.	The golden bell ringing announces the entrance of our High Priest into his church. Our High Priest is heralded when He comes. "Behold the bridegroom cometh". Furthermore, according to a writer, Neil, the heavenly blue colour of the robe unites Yashuah with His body as He imparts His Fruits and Gifts of the Spirit into us. Pomegranates represent the fruits of the Spirit and it must be interwoven with our gifts as we minister to Yahweh and His body. https://passthetoast. wordpress. com/2008/06/27/ bells-and-pomegranates/. Another writer states that Pomegranate symbolizes eternal life and fruitfulness by the redness of the seeds depicting the blood of Yeshuah.

			http://www.amazing-pomegranate-health-benefits.com/pomegranate-in-christianity.html There is a lot more to the relevance of the bell and the pomegranate which space does not permit me to record here. Definitely, it is very relevant to the 21st century believers concerning the fruitfulness of the bride and the provision that Yashuah has given us through the gifts of the Ruach Ha Kodesh (Holy Spirit).
Fine Linen Tunic	Pure White Linen	Priest"s inner clothing that atones for sexual transgression.	Pure white linen symbolizes purity of heart, soul and also covering for sexual impurity. It signifies the purity of Yeshuah Hamashiah which all believers must emulate. Yeshuah said "Ï counsel thee to buy of me pure gold tried in the fire, that thou mayest be rich; and white raiment, that thou mayest be clothed, and that thy nakedness do not appear; and anoint thine eyes with eyesalve, that thou mayest see." (Rev. 3:18)

No shoes		The priests walk barefooted standing on Holy Ground	(Word) Feet shod with the preparation of the Gospel of Peace. (Eph. 6:15) "No Shoes" symbolizes honoring Yahweh by walking according to the Holy Spirit direction and not walking in the flesh. (Rom.8:1) It also means, not leaning on Self-conceit, but leaning solely on Yahweh.
The Incense of Fragrance	Fragrance of sweet smelling incense for Yahweh's glory.	The incense is for Yahweh's enjoyment.	The Incense symbolizes the fragrance that arises from the prayers of saints who pray in the Spirit and give Yahweh glory from our lives at the altar of incense. It is the prayer offered at the will of Yahweh that the High Priest presents before Yahweh as is demonstrated on the next picture.

FURTHER COMMENTS ON THE PRIESTLY GARMENT

As you can see from the definition of the various parts of the priestly garment, each piece of the garment has an intricate relevance to the priests' characteristics and direct relevance to manner of spiritual operation in the priestly ministry. It must be noted that this elucidation is not exclusive to the high priest only or priests with high positions, such as all in the five-fold ministry. This style of life is expected from all believers who have been made kings and priests unto Yahweh his Father. (Rev. 1:6)

The priestly garment is the dressing that entitles the priest a right to the presence of Yahweh, and so the proper priestly comportment relevant to the priestly characteristics and all others stated in the bible give believers an access to the Kingdom anointing. The Kingdom Anointing is not cheap neither is it free. The grace that Yashuah secured for us, does not exonerate us from keeping His commandments and living according to the example that He has laid down for us to follow. (Rom. 6:16) The Apostles paid a high price to bring us the word of Yeshuah Hamashiah. Paul suffered imprisonment, Peter was crucified upside-down, Stephen was stoned to death yet he asked the Lord to forgive those who were stoning him. John was exiled, and James was put in a boiling oil. So what makes us think that Yahweh will reduce the price for His anointing into the Kingdom for us. If Yeshuah has granted us the kingship and priestly ministry by grace, we must ensure that we work according to His will in that position and rule and reign as kings and priests.

A further explanation about the priestly garment is expressed in the story of the marriage feast. The man who came into the marriage feast without the proper bridal garment was bound in his clothes and thrown out of the marriage feast into outer darkness where there will be gnashing of teeth. (Matt. 22:11-13). The wedding garment here symbolizes the priestly which connotes kingdom pre-requisites for access into the kingdom of Yahweh. Therefore let us take heed to how we read and understand in order to live a righteous life in all humility before Yahweh. Let us take heed not to abuse the grace of Yahweh.

The law of sin and death veiled the Holy of Holies (presence of Yahweh) from the sinner, but the death of Yashuah broke that veil from top to bottom, giving an access to all saved believers into the Holy of Holies from the Holy place. (Matt. 27:51-53) None the less, we cannot enter in with filthy hands and feet with sexual transgression and all manner of fleshly lusts. The 21st century believers have turned the grace of Yahweh into lasciviousness and the priests and laity alike practice all sorts of immoral sexual sins and the word of Yahweh is catching up on them, they are falling down dead right in the pulpit as in the days of Ananias and Sapphira. All flesh must be circumcised and pruned off unto purity. All flesh must be pruned off. Yashuah is building his church upon a rock and the gates of hell shall not prevail against it. Also He is coming back for a bride without spot or wrinkle. "That he might present it to himself a glorious church, not having spot, or wrinkle, or any such thing; but that **it should be holy and without blemish".** (Eph. 5:27)

THE MELCHIZEDEK KINGDOM ANOINTING

The anointing upon our Master Yeshuah is within the reach of believers who press into the mark of the high calling. This anointing calls for a price from believers and as we press into the spirit of holiness and righteous in

Christ. We will receive the anointing by which Yeshuah Hamashiak was anointed recorded in Acts. 10:38."

> "How God anointed Jesus of Nazareth with the Holy Ghost and with power: who went about doing good, and healing all that were oppressed of the devil; for God was with Him. And we are witnesses of all things which he did both in the land of the Jews, and in Jerusalem; whom they slew and hanged on a tree: Him God raised up the third day and showed him openly. Not to all the people but unto witnesses chosen before of God even to us who did eat and drink with him after he rose from the dead. And he commanded us to preach unto the people and testify that it is he which was ordained of God to be the Judge of quick and dead". (Acts. 10:38 – 42)

This anointing is the Melchizedek anointing which sanctifies Yeshuah's anointing apart from any other anointing. This is the reason that Yeshuah commanded the disciples to wait in the upper room for the gift of the Holy Spirit from the Father, so that He will impart the same anointing with Holy Ghost and Power upon us for the service of the Kingdom. (Acts. 1:8) Based upon that expected anointing, Yeshuah promised us that we will also do the works that He did and even greater works.

(John 14:12, 13) This anointing opens the access into the realm of the supernatural and the Kingdom of Yahweh. Unfortunately, many of the 21st century believers have disdained the spiritual manifestation of the Holy Ghost so the church is not benefitting from the supernatural that Yeshuah promised us.

At the baptism of Yeshuah Hamashiak, The heavens were opened and Hashem spoke from Heaven confirming Him, saying "This is my son in whom I am well pleased, hear ye Him". (Matt. 3:15 – 17). Even so, Hashem will open the heavens unto us as we stay connected with Him in the realm of the Spirit. Yashuah said that Hashem loves us as He loves Him and will be with us even unto the end. He said He will confirm his word in our mouth with signs and wonders following. In His name, we will cast out devils and heal the sick. (Mark 16:16-18) These are all the marks of Kingdom dwellers. It is one thing to access the Kingdom of Hashem and yet another to dwell in His presence so that His miracles continually show forth in our ministries.

KINGDOM OF HASHEM IS OUR DESTINATION

Kingdom of Hashem is our dwelling place. "He that dwelleth in the secret place of the Most High shall abide under the shadow of the Almighty. (Ps. 91:1) A perpetual abiding in the presence of the Most-High will not only assure us access into the Kingdom but will assure our ability to remain in his presence and gain the Kingdom and it will be spoken of us on that day, "Behold the tabernacle of God is with men. He will dwell with them and they shall be his people and God shall be with them and He shall be their God." (Rev. 21:5) This is the ultimate plan of our Father. He desires to manifest Himself in and through us here in the earth. The Lord Yeshuah taught us to pray "Thy Kingdom come, thy will be done on earth as it is in Heaven." Hashem is waiting for our temples to be pure and sanctified enough to accommodate His holiness so He can tabernacle within us in the Tabernacle Tent. The Tabernacle Tent is the part of the Tabernacle called the Holy Place and the Holiest of All. In reality, the Holy Place represents the heart of man. The Lord requires us to purify our hearts from all evil so He can commune with us there through his word and the golden lampstand producing the enlightenment that man needs to be spiritually minded. Beyond the Holy Place is the Holiest of all which represents the Spirit of Man. This is where man gets totally engulfed with the Godhead in the place of worship and prayer. In this realm, it is only the Spirit of God communing with the spirit of man. At this point, man is in ecstasy wrapped up or raptured in the Spirit of Yahweh. This is where Paul declared that the life that he lives is not his but Christ who lives and reigns in him. (Gal. 2:20)

THE TABERNACLE OF HASHEM

The Tabernacle of Hashem is the expected final dwelling place of Saints who have prepared themselves to abide with the Godhead as Yahshua declared in John

14:20 – 23. This is the expected New Heaven and New Earth which shall come down from heaven into the earth. (Rev. 21:1-4) The Tabernacle is made of Pure Gold which represents the purity of Hashem, Silver which represents Redemption, and various colors that represent the colors such as blue that represent heavenly sky, Purple for royalty, white for purity. I will speak more about the Tabernacle's relevance in the next book.

OBSERVATIONS/QUESTIONS

5:1.1   What did Hashem demand from the Jews?

5:1.2   Does this command also apply to believers today?

5:1.3   Why is reverencing Hashem a pre-requisite for access into the Kingdom?

5:2.1   What is the first pre-requisite to access the Kingdom of God.

5:2.2   Nicodemus was a Torah Teacher (Rabbi) in the Synagogue;why could he not understand being born again? Quote Scripture.

5:3.1.   What is the meaning of the Circumcision of the skin of our Flesh? Quote scripture.

5:3.2.   What is its relevance to the Kingdom of Hashem?

5:3.3.   What is the antitype of Circumcision of the skin of our flesh?

5:4.1.   What are the characteristics in us that are the properties of the Flesh? Quote the relevant scripture.

5:4.2   How can we mortify the fleshly lust in us and put on the new Man? Quote scriptures.

5:4.3   What is the danger of not mortifying our flesh?

5:4.4   What are the gates of hell in our lives? Quote scripture.

5:5.1   What is the importance of the Priestly garment in the New Testament dispensation?

5:5.2   What does the Mitre represent for the New Testament High Priest? Quote relevant scripture in the New Testament.

5:5.3   What is the meaning of the golden engravement on the Mitre "Holiness Unto The LORD"?

5:5.4   How vital is "Holiness Unto the LORD" in accessing the Scripture Kingdom Anointing?

5:5.5   What is the relevance of the Ephod to the New Testament Priest?

5:5.6   The names of the twelve tribes of Israel are written on the Breastplate of Judgement on the High Priest; what does it signify?

5:5.7   What does the number twelve represent?

5:5.8   What is the meaning of the Hurim and Thummim on the breastplate of the High Priest?

5:5.9   How does the New Testament Priest consult Hashem now instead of through the Lights and Perfection on the Ephod?

5:5:10 Can the N. T. Priest access the presence of Hashem without the Holy Spirit?

5:5.11 Scripture What does the Fine Linen Tunic represent?

6:1.1   Who creates access to all believers into the presence of Hashem?

6:1.2   Can anyone access the Kingdom without the Holy Spirit? Give reason and scripture.

Previews of Upcoming Books
The Kingdom of God On Earth

This will portray the Kingdom of God judicially, the spiritual Kingdom of God according to God, and the Kingdom of God in the end time with the Godhead dwelling within his Saints.

Please contact us to order more copies of our books for your friends and families.
Email. aggm.2006@yahoo.com
Facebook
www. ......
Tel. 1. 678-923-2833

REFERENCES

Neil. (2008) Bells and Pomegranates *Priest's Garment Fine Linen Tunic*, The Living Word https://passthetoast.wordpress.com/2008/06/27/bells-and-pomegranates/.

Dominici D.C. (2015) Pomegranate in Christianity - The Hope of Eternal Life, *Amazing Pomegranate Health Benefits.* http://www.amazing-pomegranate-health-benefits.com/pomegranate-in-christianity.html

Printed in the United States
By Bookmasters